"Having spent all my adult life in the realm of professional sports, I know what it's like to have victories as well as defeats. Jamie Rasmussen hits the nail on the head when he addresses the struggle we have in connecting with God. We all feel distant from God at times, and this book offers fresh help and perspective. Bringing the Bible alive in authentic and practical ways, this book will lead to more victories."

Doug Collins, Olympian, four-time NBA All-Star, College Basketball Hall of Fame, and Hall of Fame broadcaster

"With startlingly fresh insights from the book of Esther and thought-provoking, real-life examples, Pastor Jamie skillfully blazes a trail forward through dry and distant spiritual places. I love this book. It is packed with pragmatic, biblical wisdom you can put into practice immediately to get back on track. *When God Feels Far Away* invites us to explore how we can break new ground in our walk with God. It is an important reference I will return to often to be reminded of the enduring guideposts our Lord graciously places along our journey to give us hope and draw us close."

Jane E. Norton, Colorado lieutenant governor (2003–2007)

"The only thing worse than life coming apart on you is reaching out for God and sensing he's nowhere to be found. But he's there alright, and he's intimately involved in what you're up against—whether you feel his presence or not. And Jamie Rasmussen has the proof. In his new book, Jamie offers real-time, life-giving tools that empower you to draw close to God when he seems far away. Each chapter packs a wallop against despair by enabling you to not only realize the nearness of God but see his fingerprints on how he's working out your circumstances.

It's encouraging, perspective-changing, and hope-giving . . . an absolute must-read!"

Dr. Tim Kimmel, author of *Grace Filled Marriage*
and *Grace Based Parenting*

"If we are honest, who of us at one time or another has not felt a distance between us and the One who loves us most? When you finish Jamie Rasmussen's new book you will experience for yourself the promise of James to 'Draw near to God and he will draw near to you.' Read this . . . and reap!"

O. S. Hawkins, PhD, author of the bestselling Code Series of devotionals, including *The Jesus Code* and *The Bible Code*

"Who among us has not at times felt that God was distant and far away? In this book you find practical, biblical insight about these very human experiences. Jamie reveals ways to deepen our faith rather than detract from it. This is not a trite set of prescriptions but an unfolding of spiritual truths with application and encouragement."

Ted Esler, PhD, president, Missio Nexus

"This book is definitely not another 'do this and God will do that' prescription. This book is a transparent window into the life of a pastor, the book of Esther, and an awesome God who is there, even when he seems distant. Have you been there before? Jamie brings home great truth and love to our minds and hearts!"

Joe Abraham, pastor, Scranton Road Bible Church;
founder, Scranton Road Development Corporation

"In a world where corruption, crime, and coercion prevail, we need divine input to inspire and guide us to take a stand. We must be available and remember we are always on assignment. Jamie uses the story of Mordecai and Esther to illustrate what that looks like. He clearly articulates biblical trigger points that allow God to make his presence and purposes known—the antidote for when God feels far away."

Lud Golz, Pastor Emeritus, Fellowship Bible Church;
Bible teacher on Getting God's Message

"Jamie Rasmussen calls us to practice God's principles and pursue his purposes, even when God feels distant and we find ourselves in a world that's seemingly grown hostile to the gospel. His words inspire courage and offer hope for those who desire to honor God when doing so is hard."

Stephen Grcevich, MD, president and founder of Key
Ministry; author of Mental Health and the Church

"Pastor Jamie takes us on a journey to ancient Persia where the author of Esther tells the story of Israel living in exile, threatened with genocide, helpless to defend themselves—and God seems nowhere to be found. Jamie skillfully uncovers eight courageous 'ways of being' in the frightening darkness that allow Esther, Mordecai, and the Jewish people to experience the breakthrough presence of God when all seems lost. Their story, narrated through the lens of Jamie's pastoral heart, gives hope that in our own valley of the shadows, we can know God is with us—at the very moment when it seems like he's not."

J. Kevin Butcher, author of Choose and Choose Again;
executive director of Rooted Ministries, Inc.

"When you are going through tough times and God seems distant from your circumstances, I encourage you to run, not walk, to read Jamie Rasmussen's engaging and impactful book, *When God Feels Far Away*. I yearned to read more as I turned each page. A gifted writer, communicator, and teacher, Jamie shares eight key biblical pathways from the book of Esther to help us navigate divine distance when God feels far away. He weaves relatable and personal stories into each biblical application from Esther's story. We are challenged and equipped as Jamie guides us on a journey of hope with God's truth and practical application. This is a must-read book that will allow you to experience the closeness of God once again. It just doesn't get much better than that!"

Susan Miller, founder/president of Just Moved Ministry

"Jamie Rasmussen's first strength as a teacher and as a writer is his honesty. He talks about his struggles, and you realize that he is like you because you struggle too. But Jamie doesn't leave you there. He then takes you to Scripture and lays out the biblical answer to the struggles both you and he have. The result? You experience hope that things can change—and faith that you can trust God to help you deal with your struggles. If you need to feel hope and want to trust the Lord, you need to read this book."

Greg Pritchard, PhD, director of the European Leadership Forum; president of the Forum of Christian Leaders

"I am happy to recommend this book by veteran pastor Jamie Rasmussen because it is filled with wise advice on recovering and maintaining a healthy personal relationship with God, advice that comes from the words of Scripture and is illustrated with numerous fascinating stories about practical applications of these teachings in the lives of ordinary people. This book will challenge and deepen your spiritual life!"

Wayne Grudem, Distinguished Research Professor of Theology and Biblical Studies, Phoenix Seminary

"In a study of a book of the Bible that never mentions God's name, Jamie Rasmussen insightfully navigates us to clearly see God's providential engagement in the life and events surrounding Esther. Divine care is evident and will be experienced by any of us who follow what Rasmussen has mapped out for us. As it has been said, 'If you feel God is a million miles away, guess who moved?'"

Darryl DelHousaye, pastor at Redeemer Bible Church, Gilbert, Arizona

"If you have ever felt that God is distant, then put this book on your must-read list. Jamie Rasmussen skillfully invites us to get real with our experiences of distance from God rather than paper over them with religious talk. He brings the book of Esther to life with practical implications for our modern lives. This book's divine relational road map with eight solutions for spiritual dryness will refresh your faith and enrich your soul."

Richard Gray, MD, physician leader, Scottsdale, Arizona

WHEN GOD
FEELS
FAR AWAY

WHEN GOD FEELS FAR AWAY

EIGHT WAYS TO NAVIGATE DIVINE DISTANCE

JAMIE RASMUSSEN

BakerBooks

a division of Baker Publishing Group
Grand Rapids, Michigan

Published by Baker Books
a division of Baker Publishing Group
PO Box 6287, Grand Rapids, MI 49516-6287
www.bakerbooks.com

Printed in the United States of America

Library of Congress Cataloging-in-Publication Data
Names: Rasmussen, Jamie, 1964– author.
Title: When God feels far away : eight ways to navigate divine distance / Jamie Rasmussen.
Description: Grand Rapids, Michigan : Baker Books, a division of Baker Publishing Group, [2021]
Identifiers: LCCN 2021003784 | ISBN 9780801075766 (paperback) | ISBN 9781540901880 (casebound) | ISBN 9781493432929 (ebook)
Subjects: LCSH: Spirituality—Christianity. | Spiritual life—Christianity.
Classification: LCC BV4501.3 .R38 2021 | DDC 248—dc23
LC record available at https://lccn.loc.gov/2021003784

Baker Publishing Group publications use paper produced from sustainable forestry practices and post-consumer waste whenever possible.

21   22   23   24   25   26   27   7   6   5   4   3   2   1

To the late Dr. Larry Crabb,
who personally encouraged me to be honest
about long seasons when God feels far away.
And then to turn to the Bible for help.

CONTENTS

ACKNOWLEDGMENTS

My calling and vocation is that of a pastor. As a result, most of my thoughts eventually make their way into my sermons. I have been studying the Old Testament book of Esther for almost twenty years. I have preached no fewer than three lengthy sermon series on the book, spanning two different congregations. I want to thank the people of Fellowship Bible Church in Chagrin Falls, Ohio, for initially hearing my thoughts on divine distance. Their receptivity and feedback was invaluable. As well, the people of Scottsdale Bible Church in Scottsdale, Arizona, deserve a special thanks. They received two series of messages about a decade apart and helped me sharpen my understanding of how to navigate times of divine distance.

Bryan McAnally is a professional writer and pastoral colleague. His work on some of the middle chapters, combined with his skill at writing and editing, was immensely helpful. My executive assistant, Kathy Mersbach, provided administrative and editing support, without which this book would never have been finished.

Brian Vos from Baker Publishing guided this project from start to finish. His faith in the message and his wisdom along the way spurred me on. The teams at Baker have been a joy to work with, with special appreciation for Amy Nemecek, Erin Bartels, Melanie Burkhardt, and Sarah Traill.

My wife, Kim, deserves the most thanks. She gave me space to write when I needed it and profound encouragement when I would come up for breath. Mostly, she has loved me through more than three decades of navigating divine distance.

INTRODUCTION

Thirty-five years ago, I fell in love with Kim.

I was entering graduate school in Chicago, and she was halfway through her undergrad program at a school two states away. I had recently sworn off dating due to the immense complexities of collegiate romances. As far as I was concerned, I needed to look straight ahead and focus on my master's degree.

However, when love hits, it hits. And it hit. Having grown up in the same town, we had long been acquaintances. It wasn't until our college years that we each took notice of the other. We began dating the summer after I graduated from college; the proverbial sparks flew, and I was smitten. I had found the love of my life, and—miracle of miracles—she agreed!

But we had a problem. I relocated to Chicago to pursue theological training while Kim was only halfway through her college studies in southern Ohio. Her parents insisted that she finish her education there, and I couldn't pass up the opportunity to attend a world-class seminary. With full study schedules and the state of Indiana between us, we faced some new, challenging dynamics. Absent any good options, we began what became a two-year, long-distance romance.

Needless to say, the *distance* was the most obvious hurdle to overcome. It was a distance we experienced on a couple of levels. Geographically, it was precisely 321 miles. In terms of time, we were separated by a drive of four hours and fifty-four minutes in my aging 1970s sedan. Practically, our full schedules, limited time, and lack of money all contributed to keeping us far apart far too long.

Yet, even greater than the geographical hurdle was the communication hurdle. Today there is a buffet of choices for communicating. But this was the 1980s—before cell phones, FaceTime, Instagram, instant messaging, Facebook, and even email! Our only two options to bridge the distance between the rare trips were landline phone calls and written notes sent through the US mail.

Believe me, we felt every inconvenient, impractical, and impeding aspect of the distance between us.

One cool fall evening, I sat alone behind my apartment complex for one of my regular conversations with God. I was also thinking of Kim. As I looked up at the night sky, it hit me that my love could see the very same stars. As I viewed the night sky, I felt a closeness to her.

Simultaneously, I felt the distance.

The Two Decisions That Changed My Life

Let me ask you a question: Have you ever felt distant from someone you love? My guess is that you have, that you can relate to the distance I felt from Kim.

How about in your walk with God? Have you ever felt distant from God?

In my late twenties, as I sat in a therapist's office all I could think was, "You're supposed to help me feel better, not more depressed."

By almost anyone's standard, I had everything going for me. I had a great wife (yes, I married Kim!), two kids, and a third on the way. I was pastoring a growing church in a nice suburb in the Midwest. Yet my wife, my mom, the other pastors I served with, and my friends all agreed: I needed counseling. Freud once referred to depression as anger turned inward.[1] I'm not sure about all the ins and outs of how that works, but I was experiencing both anger and depression. I tried to hold it all in, stuff it down, cover it up, and keep it at bay, but emotions are tricky things, and they regularly leaked out to those around me. As one friend put it, "You need to put *us* out of *your* misery."

My counselor was a wonderful older guy who used commonsense wisdom more than book smarts. We initially worked through a few family-of-origin issues. The process took time, but it paid off. I was getting better.

From there, we moved on to spiritual things. As Christians, this counselor and I shared the same worldview. With this common frame of thinking, he broached the subject of my walk with God. Most pastors don't ever get the opportunity to talk candidly about the machinations of their own soul. Counselors, however, are paid not to freak out, or at least not to show it visibly. So I unloaded. It turns out I had some holes in the bucket of my spirituality that created a great amount of internal conflict. A friend of mine called it a "constant churning."

At the time I'd been a follower of Jesus for about twelve years. Like Paul in the Bible, I had a radical and emotional conversion. I had been going one way on the proverbial road to nowhere and Jesus made himself very clear to me. I did an about-face and headed the other way. And I never looked back. More than anything, I knew that I loved God and I loved people.

My ongoing *experience* of God, however, was a different story.

In the twelve years between my emotional and very real encounter with Jesus and the appointment with the therapist, I felt that my experience of God was too often lacking. I didn't feel him like my soul longed for, nor did I experience his movement in my life nearly as often or as consistently as I wanted.

Don't get me wrong: I read the Bible regularly, prayed all the time, worshiped him publicly and privately, attended Bible studies, hung out with other Christians, and served in the youth group. I read books on Christian meditation, contemplative prayer, healing, and the power of the Holy Spirit. I went to seminary and earned a degree in divinity. I devoted my life to serving the Lord in full-time ministry. This was my calling, and I was all in. My faithfulness, however, didn't yield what my soul longed for.

I drank from the cup I was taught to drink from, and I found myself increasingly thirsty. I was frustrated and discouraged much of the time. To borrow a phrase, I had a profound sense of "holy discontent." I had learned to *think* like a Christian and to *act* like one, but I didn't always *feel* like one.

God felt far away. I was experiencing divine distance.

When I shared this with the counselor, he said, "Well, maybe that's what the rest of your life will be like. Maybe you'll feel this way until the day you die and go to heaven. Lots of people feel like this. I hear it often."

What? That didn't sound good. Though he explained that acceptance can sometimes breed peace in the soul, his words depressed me even more.

I wasn't ready to throw in the towel.

I knew there had to be a better way, so I made two decisions that changed my life. First, I was done presenting a faux Christian image to those around me. I was done pretending. I needed to get real about my spiritual experience (or lack thereof). No matter what the cost. Life is too short to play around, especially in areas that matter.

Second, I decided that I was *not* going to accept divine distance in my walk with God. No way. I knew there had to be more. I decided I was going to spend more of my time and energy exploring the Bible, exploring my own soul, and exploring the lives of those around me.

> I had learned to **think** like a Christian and to **act** like one, but I didn't always **feel** like one. God felt far away. I was experiencing divine distance.

Honesty and exploration. These were the twin values that flowed from that defining moment in the counselor's office more than two and a half decades ago. Since then, honesty and exploration have led me to some wonderful and hard-earned discoveries.

Transcendence and Immanence

As Christians we often talk about a relationship with God through Jesus. And relationships have similarities, whether they're with other humans or with God. Every relationship involves trust, presence, communication, intimacy, give and take, visible action, and love. These are the things required to develop closeness. We long to be close to the ones we love, so it's natural to want to feel close to the one we love who is spirit.

But here's the rub: *in one sense, God is distant by his very nature.* Theologians for millennia have made a distinction between what they call the *transcendence* of God and the *immanence* of God. Simply put, transcendence is the distance of God and immanence is the closeness of God. God, because he is wholly other than us, is felt and experienced as far away. He's not of the same realm as us, as he exists in the spiritual world. We exist in the physical world, though we too have a spiritual part of us. As the psalmist says, "The LORD's throne is in heaven" (Ps. 11:4). The word *transcend* means to be above and outside, and that is a significant part of who God is.

God is transcendent. He is much higher than us. Before our fallen nature even kicks in, God is experienced as distant.

It gets more complicated. Though God wants us to experience his immanence, sin messes with our sense of nearness to him. Many times, our fallen human nature prevents us from feeling close to God. Even though God reached out to us and continues to do so in numerous ways, the part of our nature that's broken by sin prevents a connection with him.

Sin distorts reality. Similar to how mountains block cell phone reception, sin blocks our reception of God's many messages to us. Closeness becomes distance. Even though the Bible clearly reveals that Jesus came to forgive our sins and bring us into a right relationship with God, it also clearly explains that our sinful nature still regularly sabotages the closeness with God that we desperately desire.

I have yet to meet an honest Christian who doesn't relate to this problem. Every Christian feels far away from God at times.

Maybe even more often than not. We still believe in him. Our doctrine is pure. We go to church, faithfully attend small group, serve with our gifts and passions, have our daily devotions, give of our financial resources, and do our best to follow his Word.

But like myself on that cool fall evening so many years ago, looking up at the stars and longing for closeness but feeling the distance, we all want more. We thirst for more. We want to close the gap and guide our sin-blocked souls through God's transcendence to experience his immanence.

The Elephant in the Room

Here's the good news: I wrote this book to help you navigate divine distance.

I'm going to address the elephant in the room that few want to even admit, let alone talk about. Nobody likes to admit that God feels distant. That's particularly true for a Christian, especially after you've accepted Jesus into your heart, repented of known sins, trusted him through thick and thin, and given your life to him.

If you're feeling distant from God, please hear me say this: you're not alone. Your experience—or lack thereof—is universal.

> If you're feeling distant from God, please hear me say this: you're not alone.

Henry David Thoreau wrote, "In the long run men hit only what they aim at."[2] This is true of most everything in life—and it's certainly true of your approach to divine distance. Either you can accept that seasons of divine distance are par for the course, or you can make a decision, like I did, to pursue closeness with God through honesty and exploration. You must make a choice.

If you're ready to take that journey, I'll share everything I've discovered about the palette of colorful and creative solutions the Bible offers to help you repaint the canvas of your spiritual life.

There's a book tucked away in the Old Testament that deals head-on with this issue of divine distance—the story of Esther. Written at a time when God's people not only felt far from God but were far from him, the book of Esther contains eight ways to journey through seasons when God seems more behind the scenes than front and center. Each of these eight ways is proven and time-tested by God's people through the ages.

These eight ways to experience closeness with God have worked for me, and they'll work for you too. Are you ready to join me on this journey?

A DIFFERENT PATH

I have come to a place in my life where God seems hidden. It's not exactly a place of doubt. It's not exactly a spiritual dry spell. It's a place of God's removal, somehow. He doesn't seem to be right next to me. He doesn't seem to be speaking to me very loudly.

—Lauren Winner, "Into Esther"

Over the years, I've noticed a clear and common pattern of how we teach Christians to walk with God and experience him. This pattern cuts across denominational lines, and it's utilized by many serious-minded Christ followers in all kinds of settings and cultures. It looks like this:

INPUT	OUTPUT
• Study the Bible	• Wisdom/knowledge to live life
• Pray regularly	• Blessings from God
• Fellowship with other believers	• Guidance in your circumstances
• Worship publicly and privately	• Feelings of God's presence
• Serve with your gifts/passions	• Power from the Holy Spirit
• Be generous with your resources	• Motivation to persevere
• Love all people	• Personal character growth

It's an equation we use to get the most out of our faith in Jesus. It's a good equation. It's arguably biblical.

This is how many, if not most, Christians structure their walk with the Lord. We do the things the Bible tells us to do: study the Word, pray, fellowship, worship, serve, give, and love all people. As a result, we expect to see the movement of God in our midst. We expect to experience insight, blessings, guidance, good feelings, power, motivation, and changed lives (both in us and in those around us).

When this pattern works, it's fulfilling. We feel like we're batting better than average. We experience what a mentor of mine calls "God moments." All is good and fine with the world—at least in *our own* world—when it works.

Here's the rub that raises some questions: What do we do when the input-output pattern *doesn't* work?

What do we do when the power, good feelings, and God moments begin to wane?

Even more to the point: What do we do when most or all of the inputs don't seem to deliver like they once did? When prayers seem dry and unanswered? When we don't get much out of the Word? When worship doesn't engender the feelings it used to? When fellowship becomes a drag? When serving becomes an obligation and a labor? When blessings become sparse? When motivation is lacking?

What do we do when all the tried-and-true methods aren't as true as they once were? When the equation doesn't add up anymore, what do we do then?

Some people respond to these questions by saying, "Well, this doesn't happen very often. I mean, how often does the equation truly break down?"

More often than we might think. At least by biblical standards.

On no fewer than ten occasions the psalmists described their spiritual experience as God "hiding his face" from them.[1] God's immanence was blocked. The psalmists weren't *experiencing* God as they once had. And it wasn't always because the psalmist was being stubborn, rebellious, or sinful. When you read the rest of the psalms in question, where each psalmist complained of God's face being hidden, the psalmist was still pretty much applying the left side of our equation.

It's just that the right side wasn't producing like it used to. Many times, it was simply the result of a finite human soul struggling to connect with the infinite God. The psalmists' sense of divine distance was their perceived reality—God felt far away.

Israel, as a nation, experienced this same sense of estrangement. 1 Samuel 3:1 reports, "In those days the word of the LORD was rare; there were not many visions" (NIV). This was *before* Israel slipped into rebellion and apostasy. There were seasons—at times long seasons—when Israel's experience of the Lord was not like it once was. No more parting of the Red Sea. No manna from heaven. No more pillar of cloud to lead them by day or pillar of fire to guide them at night.

"The word of the LORD was rare." There was a palpable distance between the people and God. God felt far away. The equation was not adding up.

In the New Testament, we find similar seasons of divine distance. At different times, the original disciples felt confused and distant from Jesus, even when he was physically with them.

Paul the apostle, one of the most ardent and rugged followers of Jesus to ever walk this earth, had a troubling season to the point that he "despaired of life itself" (2 Cor. 1:8).

Then we have Jesus himself—the eternal Second Person of the Trinity—who cried out on the cross, "My God, my God, why have you forsaken me?" (Matt. 27:46). Though there are various explanations as to why Jesus said this, one thing they all agree on is that Jesus felt very distant from the Father at that time.

And that's the point: there are times, even seasons, when we experience divine distance. C. S. Lewis called this losing your "first fervor."[2] St. John of the Cross called this the "dark night of the soul."[3] D. Martyn Lloyd-Jones called this "spiritual depression."[4] Larry Crabb called this the "Job experience."[5]

Call it what you will, they're all getting to the same place. It's wandering-in-the-wilderness time in your walk with God.

> There's tremendous value in getting real about the times in your life when God has seemed distant, because the Bible provides hope.

Over the years since that time in the counselor's office, I've been fortunate to learn from quite a few mature and faithful followers of Jesus—spiritual veterans in the truest sense. As I have brought up this experience of divine distance, many of these friends have said their stories have lined up with the Bible's examples.

My guess is that you have your own story of divine distance. You're not alone, though it might seem like you are, because many Christians fake it, convinced they can't admit to an experience of divine distance. There's tremendous value in getting real about the times in your life when God has seemed distant, because the Bible provides hope.

Before we get into the hope the Bible provides, we need to address one more roadblock: an increasingly common response among serious-minded, well-meaning Christians that keeps many of us from finding the paths God has for us.

The Equation Is Not the Solution

As I've talked with people about what they do when God seems more behind the scenes than front and center in their lives, I often get this response: "Well Jamie, I just double down and gut it out. I spend *more* time in the Word, *more* time in prayer, add *an additional* small group study, tune into *more* Christian worship songs, volunteer *more*, and make sure I remain faithful in my giving *or even give more*. When the going gets tough, the tough get going. And I get going."

Now, I want to be clear. The things that we do to keep our walk with God going and growing are not only the right things to do but they're also what God has outlined for us in his Word to do. No right-minded follower of Jesus would try to argue differently. What we call the *spiritual disciplines*, the actions on the left side of the equation, are indispensable in forging and maintaining an intimate relationship with the Lord. We need to regularly do our spiritual exercises in order to get spiritually fit. We need to keep doing them in order to maintain spiritual vitality.

The *deficiency* in this approach to overcoming divine distance is in thinking that the equation is the be-all and end-all of your walk with God. That input-output is the final word. In reality, assuming that a *relationship* with God can ultimately be boiled down to an equation is an inadequate way of thinking. Larry Crabb rightly calls this way of approaching God "linear thinking."[6] It's the type of thinking that posits, if you do A, this leads to B as the natural result. This thinking assumes that if you perform the input then God will provide the output. Though there's an aspect to walking with God in which we "reap what we sow,"[7] that's different from saying it's the sum total of your experience with God.

Knowing God is not equational. There's more to it.

What I've discovered, and what the book of Esther reveals, is that God offers additional paths that can provide you with a more navigable trip up the mountain to him. There are ways of thinking and acting that take you beyond a linear and equational approach to God.

The problem isn't the equation. It's good and fine as it stands, but it's also not the solution.

God gives us certain activities of thought and action that we can bring into our daily spiritual activities to help us more effectively navigate seasons of divine distance.

Esther: A Story We Can Relate To

If ever there was a time in the Bible when God's people felt distant from him, it was during the time of Esther.

This story takes place around 480 BC, toward the tail end of the Old Testament. Israel had been around as a nation for more than a thousand years. After a rocky start, they eventually settled into the land. To commune with God, they obeyed God's instructions and built a mobile place of worship called the tabernacle (or tent of meeting)[8] and later the one large temple in Jerusalem where the presence of God was experienced on a regular basis.

During this adventure-filled millennium, the one thing God told them never to do was to put other things before him. To do this was called "idol worship." Israel failed completely. They consistently allowed competing aspects of other religions to vie for their affections.

As a result of their rebellion, God allowed powerful nations to come in and take over Israel. First it was the Assyrians, then the Babylonians, and finally the Persians. Nation after nation ransacked God's chosen people. But these nations didn't just inhabit Israel, they deported most of the Israelites out of their homeland. More than a million of God's chosen people were relocated to faraway places across the Middle East. Entire communities were uprooted. Homes and families were split apart in the process.

The Israelites were not just far from home geographically, they were far from home *spiritually*. In other words, they were literally far from God's presence as they had experienced it in the tabernacle and the temple.

In those times, God made his presence known through the so-called houses that were built for him. That's not to say that God never revealed himself to Israel in other ways. He did. There were appearances, angelic announcements, the words of the prophets, stone tablets, and numerous other ways God showed himself to his people. Even so, the presence of God in the tabernacle or temple was a constant for Israel in a sea of uncertainty and change. In their houses of worship, God revealed himself.

After the exile, however, Israel was far from this constant presence. If ever a people of God could claim justification for feeling far from him, they could.

As a result of this very real separation, the book of Esther is written like no other book in the Bible. What's most noticeable about Esther is what is *not* included in the story. There are four things missing in Esther that have jumped out at scholars over the years:

- *God appears to be missing.* There are no references to God. The name that every other book in the Bible mentions and expounds upon gets no mention in the book of Esther.

- *God's law appears to be missing.* There are no references to God's law or covenant. Ten chapters and not one mention of the Ten Commandments, the Mosaic covenant, or any reference to God's laws.
- *Prayer appears to be missing.* There are no direct references to prayer. An activity that the rest of the Bible references hundreds of times, something that both Judaism and Christianity build their entire understanding of a relationship with God around, is not mentioned once in this story. Talking to God is absent.
- *God's principles appear to be missing.* Concepts like God's kindness, mercy, and forgiveness—the building blocks of grace—receive no attention. It's as if someone came along and took them out at some point, yet we have ample evidence that's not the case.

Why did the author of this historical story record events this way? What was the author trying to communicate by omitting things?

Because Israel was both physically and spiritually in a far-off place when this book was written, the story was told from a perspective that screams to us about the distance the people felt from God. It was written from the vantage point of spiritual remoteness.

The story reads more like a secular account than it does a religious one. That's bothered some people over the years. The Reformer Martin Luther didn't like the book. He wrote, "I am so hostile . . . to Esther that I could wish [it] did not exist at all." It wasn't religious enough for him. It seemed too "pagan."[9] He wanted it to read more like the rest of the books in the Bible.

Shortly after the book of Esther was originally written, during a time known as the intertestamental period (between the completion of the Old Testament and the initiation of the New Testament), an anonymous editor decided the book was too nonreligious as well. Taking matters into his own hands, he added over one hundred additional verses, scattering them throughout the narrative. He spiced up the story with loads of spiritual words and imagery. He interspersed references to God, prayer, circumcision, and plenty of other spiritual imagery. It was made to read more like the Psalms than how it originally read. He attempted to force-fit the equation we talked about earlier into Esther's story. Fortunately, we have the original.[10]

Modern-Day Editors

In trying to make sense of the times when God feels far off, we tend to be like the people who tried to revise Esther to make it more appealing. Except that we do it with our own lives. We don't like it when God feels distant. We resist the seasons when he seems more behind the scenes. As a result, when God feels distant, we spice up our language to try to prove to ourselves and others that he's front and center in our lives. We sing louder and talk more. We act more spiritual than how we feel. Like myself in the counselor's office years ago, we're reticent to admit the season we're in.

Is it any wonder why we feel fake or empty at times? It's time to end the charades.

I believe the original writing of the story of Esther contains exactly what we need to get honest about divine distance and to begin exploring it. The story doesn't need editing. The original raw and real version will do.

The author wants us to feel what a story line reads like when God is more behind the scenes. The author wants us to identify with times when God seems distant from our everyday circumstances. Esther's story is designed to help us realize there are times in a fallen world, even lengthy seasons, when God seems distant, remote, and inactive. It's an invitation to get honest and explore.

The Rest of the Story

Esther's story invites us to explore some pathways few choose to take. A road less traveled and less foot worn. A road filled with tremendous hope for those of us who get real and desire to get God in a way our souls long for.

Esther does more than simply chronicle what it feels like when God seems distant. It reveals that God is present even when he feels far way. He's still active despite seeming inactive. He's there, doing what only he can do, albeit behind the scenes. Someone once said, "A coincidence is a small miracle in which God chose to remain anonymous." The story of Esther is filled with lots of thinly veiled "coincidences." They all have a divine origin. God is on the move.

With faith, that can become the story of our lives as well.

WAY 1

Trusting in God's Providence

Safia offered her own prayer. Silence was her only answer,
but it still gave her comfort.

—James Rollins, *Sandstorm*

Everyone needs to be challenged when it comes to faith. We all need to be nudged now and then to keep us sharp and on track as to the composition and makeup of our faith.

I remember one of the first times my faith was challenged. It happened when I was at college as a young follower of Jesus. As I passed dozens of other students in the open courtyard on their way to or from class, I hardly noticed them. I was deep in thought.

I was in my second year of college, studying religion and psychology. A few months earlier I was introduced to an age-old dilemma in theology and philosophy: God's sovereignty and our free will. Are the courses of human lives *ultimately* decided by God's will or human choices? Obviously, both are in play. But in the final analysis, whose will and determination has more sway? God's or ours? I had recently read a couple of lengthy books that argued for each side. It bothered me that the answer wasn't easy.

My face must have given me away, because when I walked by one of my professors, he stopped me. As an Army officer turned theologian, he was known for his intelligence, wit, and outgoing personality. Getting my attention, he asked, "Rasmussen! Why the long face? What has you so tightly wound today?"

I told him I couldn't make sense of the divine/human conundrum. I'll never forget his response, "Oh, that's not so difficult. Think of it this way. At the end of the day, who do you want to be more in charge of it all, God or us? Who do you want to ultimately be in control? Who do you think should have the final say? A sovereign, all-knowing, all-good, all-powerful God, or you and me?"

Sometimes the simplest ways of looking at things are the best ways. I knew the answer to this one. I voted for God. This was a game changer for me in how I viewed God, myself, and the realities around me. It would also change how I utilized and focused my faith. We all need to be challenged and nudged now and then.

The Foundation Is Faith

Have you noticed that people today are high on faith?

Faith is a badge of honor for all kinds of people from media personalities to Hollywood celebrities to politicians to doctors to country-club elites. It goes like this:

"You just got to have a little faith."

"I'm a person of faith."

"Faith will get you through it."

"Keep the faith."

It's vogue to talk about faith today. No one judges you for having it or mentioning it in polite society. I'm glad our culture is warm to this. It's a good thing.

The Bible repeatedly affirms the value of faith. Jesus said all you need is "faith as small as a mustard seed" and you will move mountains (Matt. 17:20 NIV). The book of Hebrews says, "And without faith it is impossible to please God" (Heb. 11:6 NIV). Paul the apostle said that of the three primary things that matter in life, faith makes the list (see 1 Cor. 13:13). He went on to call faith a "gift of God" (Eph. 2:8). The Bible repeatedly plays the tune of faith. It's a song we are designed to dance to in life.

You Hit What You Aim At

What's lacking in our culture's love of faith is both the right *object* of faith, as well as *what we are specifically trusting* in when it comes to the object of our faith. While it's a good and wonderful thing to believe in the power of faith, that's only the beginning. There must be both a *right direction* and a *solid substance* to our faith.

Philosophically, faith is trusting in something or someone. It's marked by leaning, resting, and depending. Some say that faith is a crutch. In a sense it is. By its very nature, faith places weight on something in order to get the most out of it. We use faith to help us walk and not limp. Faith gives us confidence to move on and up in life. We all use it, and this is why faith is a universally agreed upon quality needed in life.

So, what about the *object(s)* of your faith? Where should you place your faith?

While culture praises the virtues of faith, there's no clear consensus on the object(s). Some mean faith in yourself. That's been popular since the rise of the self-obsessed Me Generation of baby boomers.

Others mean faith in fate. We're all familiar with the logic: "Everything happens for a reason."

Still others mean faith in the goodness of humanity in general, suggesting that the good in others will outweigh the bad.

The list is endless: faith in technology, faith in science, faith in doctors, faith in the human body to heal itself. The smorgasbord of faith objects has become so overwhelming that some people today ultimately hit the reset button and simply opt for faith in the power of faith with no object declared: "You've just got to have faith."

With so many faith options, it's important to realize that every human being has a finite capacity for faith. The Bible affirms this.[1] A person's faith can go in only so many directions. We all must choose carefully who or what we're going to trust in and lean on the most.

Years ago, when I was talking about faith with a close childhood friend, he declared that he believed in God, but only in a general sort of way. He called himself a "liberal believer in God." He didn't want to go any further than this. He didn't want to get too radical. I asked him what that's done for him in life. He said, "Not much."

You hit what you aim at. We need to choose the direction and object of our faith carefully and wisely.

Christianity maintains that it's through faith in Jesus that a person enters into an eternal relationship with God. It further maintains that it's faith in the *person* and *work* of Jesus that counts. His person as the eternal Son of God and his work on the cross to secure the forgiveness of our sin. Both the *object* of faith (the person of Jesus), as well as *what we are specifically trusting* in when it comes to the object (Jesus's work on the cross) are both clearly defined.

This is the foundation of faith from which all else flows. To believe in Jesus as Savior and Lord is critical. It's how one enters into a relationship with God.

Aim for Providence

Building upon the foundation of faith in Jesus, a further kind of faith is needed and shown in the story of Esther. This further faith is the one that I was nudged into back in college, and it allows one to begin navigating times of divine distance. It's faith in the *providence* of God.

Before we define providence, let's review the book of Esther. The story involves four main players:

- Ahasuerus, the king of Persia
- Haman, the king's second-in-command
- Esther, a beautiful young Jewish woman orphaned as a child
- Mordecai, Esther's cousin and caretaker

It's late in the Old Testament period, and Esther and many of her fellow Israelites are living in exile in various places in Persia (modern-day Iran). The first chapter sets the tone of the story by describing the culture at that time. It could have been ripped from today's headlines. The culture of Esther's day is described in four ways:

- Secular—void of the religious influences the Jewish people were used to
- Hedonistic—obsessed with material things, food, and the pleasures of the good life
- Gender objectification—women were viewed as objects of pleasure and desire
- Politically dysfunctional—Persia was a monarchy in which the king issued decrees, and his decrees were law

It was this cultural setting, combined with being far away from their spiritual home, that caused God's people to feel distant from him.

Toward the end of chapter 1, these four cultural pillars converge in a way that will change the lives of all four players. The king had a lavish party where he drank too much wine. He made the not-so-wise decision of summoning his wife, Queen Vashti, to the party so his guests could gawk at her beauty. Her refusal enraged the king, so he issued a royal edict that banished Vashti from his presence and removed her as queen. The effect was like divorcing her. As a result, Ahasuerus was now on the hunt for a new queen. Through a strange turn of events, the king chose a beautiful Jewish woman, Esther. She married the king of Persia and became the queen.

The king had no idea that Esther was Jewish. Nor did he care at that point. He married her because she was gorgeous. But shortly after their marriage, Haman, the king's second-in-command, hatched a plot because of his hatred of the Jews.

Esther's cousin, Mordecai, told her about Haman's plan to completely exterminate the Jews from Persia, and though she wanted to use her influence to get the king to do something about this, it wasn't easy.

In that gender-objectifying, politically dysfunctional culture, a person didn't just waltz in and start talking to the king. Not even the queen. A person had to be formally invited to appear before the king in a special chamber designed for pleading one's case. Breaking this rule promised serious consequences—life and death consequences. Somehow, Esther had to get in to see the king to get him to stop Haman's crazy plan to kill all of her people. She didn't know how to do it without losing her life, so she told Mordecai that there wasn't much she could do. It was too risky.

At this point in the story, the book's primary theme passage comes into focus. Mordecai responds to Esther's throwing in the towel, saying, "For if you keep silent at this time, relief and deliverance will rise for the Jews from another place, but you and your father's house will perish. And who knows whether you have not come to the kingdom for such a time as this?" (Esther 4:14).

Let's not miss what's going on here. Mordecai conveys to Esther that God, who's never mentioned in the story, will provide deliverance for the Jews. "Relief and deliverance will arise for the Jews from another place."

From where? From what place?

The history of the Jewish people screams to them at this moment, "God's place!" God will come through! Mordecai tells Esther to *believe* and *trust* in that promise. Though God was seemingly far away and felt as distant, he could be trusted here.

Further, Mordecai asks Esther to consider a piercing question: Why, out of millions of women, would King Ahasuerus choose her, an exiled Jewish woman, to be his queen at precisely the time when she could be in a position to save her people? Coincidence? Mordecai thinks not. He speaks as though he can see an invisible, guiding hand positioning the chess pieces on the board.

It's God. And he is positioning them to win.

This single verse in Esther, veiled as it is, points to God. This verse points to a certain attribute of God that theologians call providence. He's the one in ultimate control of things. He has a plan and he's working it out, albeit behind the scenes. As one scholar wrote, "Only one conclusion can be reached . . . God was behind it all. . . . The most pervasive teaching in the entire book is the importance and extent of God's providence—his sovereignty over nature, nations and individuals."[2]

The events swirling around Mordecai and Esther were chaotic. They were looking to survive in a crazy culture. The circumstances felt like God was out of the picture. Things were bleak at first and only got bleaker.

But God's control was also in play. Mordecai was supremely confident of this. God would not let his people down. And Esther needed to place her faith fully and squarely in the providence of God. Trusting God would be the key to her saving her people. Further, this specific kind of faith—faith in the providence of God—would be the foundation for navigating the divine distance they all felt.

Who or What Is Ultimately in Control?

God's providence is defined as "God's faithful and effective care and guidance of everything which He has made toward the end which He has chosen."[3] Our faith in God's providence is built upon the reality that there is a plan for this world, one that ultimately cannot be thwarted because it's rooted in an all-knowing, all-powerful God. According to his providential plan, God uses everything, even the bad things, to accomplish his purposes for his people.

It's faith in this aspect of God's character and actions that's regularly emphasized in the Bible. This emphasis is for good reason, as it guides our souls from the chaos of this fallen world to a sense of God's ultimate control.

> **According to his providential plan, God uses everything, even the bad things, to accomplish his purposes for his people.**

Long after the time of Esther, when Paul the apostle was trying to get Greek philosophers to embrace God for who he is, he appealed to the twin ideas of God as Creator and God as providential. He said, "And he [God] made from one man every nation of mankind to live on all the face of the earth, having determined allotted periods and the boundaries of their dwelling place, that they should seek God, and perhaps feel their way toward him and find him. Yet he is actually not far from each one of us" (Acts 17:26–27).

Let that sink in. Where you were born, the exact time in history it happened, the city you live in, the house you have, and the career path you chose—all of it falls within the "appointed times" and "boundaries" determined by God. He functions this way so that you might know he is real and seek to know him.

Jesus affirmed this same aspect of God's character when he said, "Are not two sparrows sold for a penny? And not one of them will fall to the ground apart from your Father. . . . Fear not, therefore; you are of more value than many sparrows" (Matt. 10:29, 31). The illustration is so simple it's almost comical. Our fears are swallowed up in the providence of God. Jesus logically reasoned that if God cares about small birds and oversees their lives, he certainly cares about you and me. He is capable of ultimately guiding and overseeing our lives as well.

The idea of God's providence is neatly summarized in Paul's famous words in the book of Romans, "And we know that for those who love God all things work together for good, for those who are called according to his purpose" (Rom. 8:28). Two things converge here: God's ability to make "all things work together for good" and our willingness to trust in his providence, "his purpose." God's capability of managing the chessboard of our lives meets our courage of believing in his ability to do so. When these two things come together, they become the sparks that ignite the kind of walk with God that can get us through the darkest times.

Just as that wonderful, witty professor guided me on the day I bumped into him when walking across the college courtyard, we each have to decide in life who or what is *ultimately* in control of things. Is it us? Is it fate? Is it the machinations of our modern, technologically advanced culture?

Or is it a personal and providential God? The creator, sustainer, ruler, and redeemer of our souls? The answer to this question determines the direction and substance of our faith. It also becomes a powerful force in determining what kind of experience we have with God, especially when he feels far away.

Faith Itself Is the Experience

Faith in the providence of God is vastly more important than many of us realize. When it comes to experiencing God, what we often fail to understand is that *faith is its own experience*.

That's particularly important when the other experiences wane—when prayer, worship, service, giving, fellowship, and our daily devotions don't produce the feelings and results they once did. Daring to laser focus our faith on God as its object, and then specifically banking on his providential care of our lives, becomes the proverbial "North Star" for navigating times when life is out of control. Faith itself becomes the experience.

I want to be clear: I'm not merely arguing that faith *leads to* other experiences (though this is certainly true). Faith in Jesus, faith in God's providence, and faith in other aspects of God's character leads to wonderful experiences in the Word, prayer, worship, service, fellowship, giving, and more. Faith leads to blessings, guidance, wisdom, and all the other "results" we noted in the equation earlier. Faith is indeed the fuel that drives your walk with the Lord, leading to many wonderful experiences with him.

> Before it takes you along glorious paths leading to other experiences, faith carries its own blessings. Faith becomes its own blessing.

We need to realize, however, that faith as a *stand-alone entity* is an experience. Before it takes you along glorious paths leading to other experiences, faith carries its own blessings. Faith becomes its own blessing.

That's important because many times we bemoan and begrudge the fact that we aren't experiencing God like we used to,

45

when God has placed right before us opportunities to know him through leaning on his providence. Willfully and consciously banking on this attribute of God contains multiple benefits that become core to experiencing God in times when he feels far away.

Providence Delivers

There are three primary experiences we have with God nestled *within* a deeply held trust in his providence. They're the kind of experiences that blow through the effects of a runaway culture around us.

1. God's Providence Gives Comfort

The famous Heidelberg Catechism, an organized set of Christian beliefs used by churches in Germany shortly after the Reformation, opens with this profound question and answer:

> Q. What is your only comfort in life and death?
>
> A. That I am not my own, but belong with body and soul, both in life and in death, to my faithful Savior Jesus Christ. . . . He also preserves me in such a way that without the will of my heavenly Father not a hair can fall from my head; indeed, all things must work together for my salvation.[4]

God's providence gives amazing comfort. His providence lets us know that he's in control and has us in his grip no matter what we might be going through. No matter how crazy things get around us, we're comforted by the fact that God has a plan and that his plan will not be stopped.

A few years ago, when one of my teenage children was going through a dark period in life, our family was in turmoil. I've said for years that with God's help I can handle anything that befalls me. But when one of my kids is hurting, my life is wrecked. My wife felt the same way. I remember drives to work when I normally would listen to music or talk radio to clear my head, but during this season no music or discussion would soothe the ache in my soul. It was a difficult time for all of us. I was deeply concerned for my child, and I was not sure how it would all work out. It was a consuming thing for my wife and me.

At one point, I began to focus on the providence of God. I embraced the reality that, though things looked dark, God still had this under control. He wasn't surprised at my kid's struggles. He wasn't caught off guard. He knew this would happen before any of it came to pass. He also had a plan for my child—his child. God's promise, spoken through the prophet Jeremiah, came to mind: "For I know the plans I have for you, declares the LORD, plans for welfare and not for evil, to give you a future and a hope" (Jer. 29:11). Though this promise was given specifically to Israel in their time of darkness, I didn't mind embracing it for my family.

A calming effect washed over me. It was palpable. God's control over the circumstances was greater than my child's choices. I trusted that as human will careened into God's will, God's good will would prevail. My wife joined me in embracing this promise. She bought a plaque with this verse from the prophet Jeremiah and displayed it prominently in our house. Every time we glanced at it and embraced the promise, we were comforted.

As the psalmist wrote, "Weeping may tarry for the night, but joy comes with the morning" (Ps. 30:5). Eventually the darkness passed, and our child saw daylight once again. Though it took time, good choices were made, and healing occurred. Over time, joy was restored. It was a joy born of comfort and contained in a stubborn embrace of God's providence. It works that way.

Are you going through a similar scenario where one of your loved ones is in a dark place? Or are you facing a darkness of your own, brought on by circumstances you didn't see coming?

If so, you understand all too well that a fallen world can wreak havoc on your God-created soul. Yet, you can experience comfort that is rooted in faith in the promise of God as you embrace his providence.

2. God's Providence Gives Hope

Hope is an experience contained within a trust in God's providence. I define hope as, "The ability to see beyond your present circumstances to that which is unseen." Hope is a paradox in that it sees what is not seen. Like most paradoxes, however, there's truth in it. In hope, we look to the horizons of our lives, and though we might see only storm clouds, we know who controls the storm. Even though we have no idea how it's all going to play out, we know who has this under control.

There's a powerful description of Abraham's experience of faith tucked away in the book of Romans. Paul reflects on Abraham's life and how things didn't look very hopeful. Abraham was almost one hundred years old, and his wife Sarah was ninety. Many years earlier, God had promised them a son who would carry on Abraham's family line and become a great nation, but Sarah wasn't able to become pregnant. According to Guinness World Records, the oldest woman to give birth in our modern age was sixty-six, and this was only with the help of in vitro fertilization.[5] At age ninety, Sarah didn't stand a chance.

This is how Romans 4:18 describes the setting: "Against all hope, Abraham in hope believed and so became the father of many nations" (NIV). It's a play on words. In hope, against all hope, Abraham believed that God would come through. And God did. A ninety-year-old woman became pregnant and gave birth to a son. They called him Isaac, which in Hebrew means "laughter," because Sarah had laughed when Abraham told her that God was going to give them a son.

In the classic movie *The Shawshank Redemption*, the main character, Andy, is wrongly convicted and placed in prison for decades. There, he becomes friends with another inmate, Red. Throughout the movie, the two men disagree on the nature and power of hope. Red believes hope is dangerous as it leads to crippling disappointment when it goes unrealized or unfulfilled. Andy, though, believes that hope keeps one's spirit alive and vital. After years of incarceration, Andy finally escapes. Red serves out his full term and is released a few years later. After his release, Red finds a note from Andy that says, "Hope is a good thing, maybe the best of the things, and no good thing ever dies."[6]

Imagine how this works for those who trust in the never-swaying providence of God. The logic is flawless: if God has a plan for our lives, *and* if God is in control, then there is always a reason to hope. Hope lives in the souls of those who know what God is like and lean on him. Hope is contained within a faith that holds fast to the providence of God. As the Bible declares, "On him we have set our hope that he will continue to deliver us" (2 Cor. 1:10 NIV).

Relying on the providence of God provides the experience of hope.

3. God's Providence Gives Strength

A reliance on God's providence gives us strength. It's a strength to persevere, to not freak out, and to stay the course. It's a strength to not take matters into your own hands and to rest in God's providential actions, timetable, and control. As the psalmist put it, "Let the nations be glad and sing for joy, for you judge the peoples with equity and guide the nations upon earth" (Ps. 67:4). Gladness and joy should be your actions in light of his providence, not getting ahead of God and doing your own thing.

This is important. One of the great temptations when God feels far away is to take matters into our own hands. We figure that if God is going to be distant, we'll return the favor. As a result, we make decisions and engage in actions that are in conflict with a life submitted to the Lord. This type of independent reaction is an inherent vulnerability during seasons of divine distance.

Looking back at the story of Abraham and Sarah, we see that they struggled with this. At one point, when they were impatient with God's timing, they decided to take matters into their own hands. They decided that Abraham would conceive a child with Sarah's servant Hagar. Hagar became pregnant and gave birth to Ishmael, but he wasn't the son God had promised Abraham, and God let Abraham and Sarah know this. To add insult to injury, jealousy and strife arose between Sarah and Hagar because now they were both tied to Abraham. It was only through a reenergized faith in God's providential promise that Abraham found the strength to stop taking matters into his own hands and trust in God's plan.

When I look back on the dark period when my own family was in chaos, I also experienced a temptation to try to get ahead of God. There was a strong desire to try to fix the situation on my own without God's intervention. However, spiritual and relational things in life take time. Such matters are more like crockpots than microwaves. Though it wasn't easy to rest in God's control, I found it was a much better choice than trying some of my half-baked schemes. Understanding and relying on God's providence gave me the strength to not move ahead of God. Strength to hang in there and persevere.

Are there some situations in your life right now that you're tempted to try to control? Are there things that God's asking you to let go of and turn over to him?

With a focused faith on his providence, you can find strength.

Providence Eats Culture for Breakfast

The message of Esther is that God's providence is worth trusting. His providence is the foundation of the entire story.

Likewise, God's providence is more than enough to deal with everything going on around you. From a crazy culture to the problems of your life to seasons of divine distance, embracing this outpouring of God's provision will provide the comfort, hope, and strength you need to not simply survive but thrive.

When I was a little boy, I slept soundly. As I reflect on this as an adult, I realize that my childhood psyche was settled in great part due to the presence of my father in the house. My dad was always in control. He worked hard during the day, provided well for his family, was home at the end of the day for dinner, and locked up the house at night. I felt secure and safe within our house.

Here's what's strange: my bedroom was the *farthest* of all the kids' rooms from my parents' bedroom. It was on the

> **Embracing this outpouring of God's provision will provide the comfort, hope, and strength you need to not simply survive but thrive.**

complete opposite corner of the house—down the hall, hard left turn, and then straight ahead. But while their room was physically *distant* from my bedroom, I nevertheless felt safe. Why? My father was in the house and in control. My trust in this gave me comfort, hope, and strength even through the distance. My trust in my father's control allowed me to feel his presence despite the distance between us during the night.

It's easy in our fallen world and turbulent culture to feel like things are out of control. It's likewise easy to feel far from God at times. But he's still in the house.

We can rest safe and secure if we'll trust that he's in control. When it comes to navigating the divine distance we experience in our lives, this trust in God's providence becomes the foundation upon which all else is built.

WAY 2

Choosing Humility over Pride

He that is humble ever shall have God to be his guide.

—John Bunyan

You're fired."

That two-word statement has to be one of the most damaging things a person can hear. Those words often come unexpectedly. It may be more flowery to be told "your services are no longer needed," or "your time with us has come to an end," but the result is just as unsettling.

Believe me, I've been there. Getting fired was a difficult and deflating experience that I'll never forget.

During seminary, I worked for a national youth organization as a campus leader. My job was to put on weekly events that were fun for teenagers: burger bashes, sporting activities, club meetings, and the like. As I engaged with students at events, I was supposed to initiate conversations about God.

On paper, the job seemed like a good fit. I was relatively new to my Christian faith. I was studying to be a pastor, and I was only a few years out of high school myself. I still had the cool factor that my kids now tell me is gone.

One sunny afternoon, my supervisor sent me to a varsity soccer practice to follow up on one of our events. The entire soccer team had shown up to chow down on burgers, and now I was going to take the next step and hang out with them on their turf. The problem was, it was there that all my anxieties jumped out of the shadows. There was no question—loving God and people were my strong suits. Still, I was an insecure mess who cared way too much about what others thought of me. I struggled with my own adolescent hangover of wanting to fit in and be liked. In the parking lot at the practice, I sat in my car sweating as I saw the kids kicking the ball around. My fears were in overdrive. What if they thought I was weird? What if they rejected me? What if all this God stuff drove them away? I was terrified of their response to my presence as the religious guy there to talk about God. With my fears in tow, I drove away, hoping nobody noticed.

I hate to admit it, but this wasn't the only time I chickened out. Soon enough, my supervisors observed the disconnect between the events I put on and my lack of spiritual engagement with the teens. My insecurities were obvious, and my lack of relational courage was evident. The report went all the way to the top, and the regional head of the organization set up a meeting for us to have lunch and talk. This conversation had the capacity to either make or break my fragile spirit.

At lunch, the regional director outlined my lackluster performance, and we agreed that I needed relational courage to succeed. He said they still thought I had the goods for ministry, but I would need some strong mentoring to get there. He told me that if I was willing to put off seminary for a while and come on full-time staff with the organization, it would give them the time they needed to help me grow. They were willing to invest in me.

I told the regional director that my father was graciously paying for me to be in graduate school with the one proviso that I finish. If I quit, the funding would dry up, so I couldn't quit school.

He then said, "You can consider this your last day with us."

The disgrace I felt in my shame-ridden soul was overwhelming.

I didn't know what to say. I wanted to crawl under the table and hide. More than that, I wanted to get out of there as fast as I could. Before I could crawl or run, however, this man said something to me that changed everything. He said, "Here is what I know, Jamie. You will work through many of your insecurities and you'll make a great pastor someday. I believe that. In fact, I'm sure of it. God has his hand on you. And in the years ahead when I hear of all that God is doing in and through you, I will say to the person next to me, 'We had a hand in that man's life. Look at him now.'"

It brings tears to my eyes as I write this now. Even as he fired me, his words of profound affirmation became words that would set the course for my healing.

As I've reflected on that lunch over the years, it continues to amaze me how *humble* this man was. He had the power to rip me to shreds. He had the power to put me in my place and tell me to either get with the program or get out. Over the years, I've heard firsthand horror stories of prideful people in authority using their power to run others over.

The regional director was different. He was centered in his own sense of self. He was centered in his understanding of who God is and who he was. He was *humble* in character, yet he was an able and strong leader. It was his humility that allowed me to receive his words of release, along with his words of affirmation. Absent this humility, I'm certain my defenses would have kicked in and my youthful tongue would've lashed out. His humility drew me to him, even as he was firing me for things I did not fully understand at that time.

> Humility works that way. It breaks down defenses. It builds bridges. It draws others in. It makes others want to be with us —and us with them.

Humility works that way. It breaks down defenses. It builds bridges. It draws others in. It makes others want to be with us—and us with them. Even when we must do and say difficult things, humility stands the best chance at keeping the connection strong and stable.

Most of us have had experiences in life that have revealed this to us. A parent whose humility drew us to them. A spouse whose humility became a healing agent in our lives. A friend or coworker whose humility created a safe place for us to be ourselves. Or, like with me, a boss whose humility paved the way for healing and growth. We have experienced firsthand this bridge-building aspect of humility.

Humility works on the human level. We shouldn't be surprised, then, that it works even more so on the divine level. Humility is a pathway to navigating divine distance because it draws us close.

A Contrast in Character

In the story of Esther, we see this theme of humility introduced early on. Building upon the already established trait of trust in God's providence, the narrator of the story paints a picture of two very different kinds of character, which even today are critical for navigating times of divine distance. The story reveals that there's a *choice* to be made when God feels far away. It's a choice between a character built upon pride or a character built upon humility.

Each choice leads to a very different experience with God.

Wounded pride explains why the king banished Queen Vashti for her refusal to be paraded in front of his dinner party. His young attendants soothed his pride by offering to canvass his kingdom for beautiful young virgins, gather them at the citadel in Susa, and place them in the king's harem. There they'd be groomed under the watchful eye of Hegai, the king's eunuch, and compete to be chosen as the next queen. When he heard this idea, "This pleased the king, and he did so" (Esther 2:4).

Remember, the four pillars that held up the Persian culture of that time were secularism, hedonism, gender objectification, and political dysfunction. All four are here in spades. There's no mention of anything religious. Everything centered around the pleasure of the king. Women were merely objects for the king's pleasure. And the advice given to the king was purely designed to play to his ego.

More to the point, it's all about *pride*. Specifically, the king's pride. His pride had been wounded when Vashti wouldn't appease his hedonistic desires. Now his pride led the way as he pursued his own pleasures.

Pride occurs when we unduly assert the self. Pride is about unnecessarily inflating certain aspects of ourselves. It's thinking more highly of ourselves than is warranted, having an unrealistic view of ourselves. Pride is the culprit when we make everything about us to the exclusion of others and even God. Pride is the ultimate self-centeredness. All of us recognize pride when we see it. Clearly, King Ahasuerus was fueled by high-octane pride.

Into this pride-filled situation entered Esther and her cousin, Mordecai. The contrast couldn't be more stark between their character and the character of the king. Throughout the rest of chapter 2, there are multiple descriptions of *humility* that act as neon signs that position it opposite to the king's pride. For example, our two players are introduced this way:

> He [Mordecai] was bringing up Hadassah, that is Esther, the daughter of his uncle, for she had neither father nor mother. The young woman had a beautiful figure and was lovely to look at, and when her father and her mother died, Mordecai took her as his own daughter. (2:7)

Though Mordecai is a cousin to Esther, he adopts her as his daughter and treats her with care and respect. The king was never known for caring for needy family members—only for using people for his own desires. Mordecai, thinking not of himself, took Esther in and looked after her in a purely fatherly way. In contrast to pride's inflated view of self, humility has an uninflated view of one's self.

As the famous nineteenth-century preacher Charles Spurgeon said, "Humility is to make a right estimate of one's self."[1] The New Testament affirms this definition of humility with the warning, "Do not think of yourself more highly than you ought, but rather think of yourself with sober judgment" (Rom. 12:3 NIV).

Mordecai had this down flat. He didn't see himself as an entitled cousin to Esther, but as a protector and father figure. He didn't take advantage of this situation in a way that could have benefited him and his ego. Rather than choosing a romantic path (which was more common in the cultures at that time), he chose a paternal one. Humility—a right estimation of himself—enabled Mordecai to have this view.

We see a further example of such self-assessing humility with Esther. When the king's attendant rounded up the most beautiful women in Persia, he put them through an entire year of what can be best described as an extreme makeover. The text says each woman went through "the regular period of their beautifying, six months with oil of myrrh and six months with spices and ointments for women" (Esther 2:12). Esther was already beautiful, however. She had a "beautiful figure" and was "lovely to look at" (2:7).

When it came time for her to experience this makeover and go see the king, it's interesting what happens next: "When the turn came for Esther . . . to go in to the king, she asked for nothing except what Hegai the king's eunuch, who had charge of the women, advised. Now Esther was winning favor in the eyes of all who saw her" (Esther 2:15). What we don't want to miss here is that Esther was comfortable in her own skin. She was humble about her own looks. She didn't feel that she needed anything more to enhance them. And in a move of further humility, she listened to wise counsel from a guy who knew the king. There's no pride to be found here, though she had every reason to be proud.

Mordecai and Esther both reveal they had a right estimation of themselves. They knew the gifts they had to offer this world, and they knew their limitations. No fakery needed. Mordecai was a protector and sage to his young cousin. He was secure in his role. There was no need to take this any further. Esther probably could have been named Miss Universe 480 BC, yet she wanted no more than what was needed to help her people. Contrast that with the king, who did not restrain his pride in seeking personal pleasure and advancement. We clearly see the line drawn. It's character built upon pride set against character built upon humility.

Providence Smiles on Humility

This is an extremely important principle to grasp as we work through times when God feels far away. Many people in our fast-paced, success-focused, highly competitive modern culture have little room for humility. They see it as something for the weak. Something that will hold them down, take the edge off their drive and ambition. Something that will come between them and their goals. Nothing could be further from the truth. As the story of Esther progresses, we'll see that both Mordecai and Esther exhibit profound strength and stamina. Their leadership and wisdom will become evident—in and through their humility, not despite it.

Most importantly, however, it'll be their humility that will allow them to hang in there and experience God once again. Humility is one of the foundational tools God has given us to navigate times of divine distance. Just as humility can build bridges on a human level, it builds similar ones on the divine level. God loves humility and will use it to draw us close to him, especially when we feel far away.

James 4:6 declares, "But he [God] gives more grace. Therefore, it says, 'God opposes the proud but gives grace to the humble.'" Notice that this passage has a positive-negative-positive flow to it. It begins positively by telling us that God desires to give us more grace. Grace is God's favor. It is his blessing. We receive grace anytime he shows us his love and reveals his activity in our lives. The result of grace is almost always a rich sense of his presence. How could it not be?

Now for the negative part. This passage goes on to say that there's one primary and certain thing that will block this grace, and that's pride. God is repelled by pride. He's not drawn to us when we're full of pride. As we have seen, pride is all about self. It's about unduly uplifting ourselves and being full of ourselves. God is not impressed with this. Pride gets in the way of his goodness and centrality in our lives. When it comes to God, pride is a presence repellant. Our experience of God's presence comes through his grace, but our pride blocks that experience.

> When you feel far from God, pride may not always be the culprit, but humility is always the solution.

What can be done about this? The James passage ends on another positive note: *humility*. God gives his grace (his favor, blessings, and sense of his presence) to those who demonstrate humility (the right estimation of who they are).

This truth brings sight-giving clarity. When you feel far from God, pride may not always be the culprit, but humility is always the solution.

God's drawn to those who know their place in the grand scheme of things. He's drawn to those who know who he is (providential and worthy of our faith), know who they are (gifted, but not *the* gift to humankind), and learn to live in light of these realities. In a very real way, humility places you directly in the pathway of God's grace. It places you in the prime position to experience him once again. Humility allows you to be in the right place at the right time when it comes to God. Humility unleashes an experience of his grace in your life.

Esther and her people will see the light of day again. They are going to navigate divine distance and celebrate the goodness of God in their midst. But make no mistake, whatever goodness they will experience from God in their dire circumstances, it will be founded upon their choice of humility. Providence smiles on humility.

A Lesson from Nature

Have you ever paused to look at an elaborate fish tank in a public aquarium or fine restaurant? Two of the more common types of fish that people tend to marvel at are the puffer fish and angelfish. They're both unique and beautiful species of fish. They're also very different.

Puffer fish, also known as blowfish, appear normal at first glance, but they're able to inflate themselves like a big balloon. They do this by filling their elastic stomachs with water and air. It's a defense mechanism that makes them look two to three times their normal size. And though it looks fascinating and beautiful, it's deceptive. Most puffer fish contain a toxic substance that makes them taste foul to other fish. The toxin is also highly lethal. There's enough toxin in one puffer fish to kill thirty adult humans. It's twelve hundred times more deadly than cyanide, and there's no known antidote.

The point: puffer fish are fine to look at, but it's wise to avoid them. Most fish in the ocean know this.

Angelfish are the opposite. Angelfish are also fascinating and beautiful, but they're relatively calm and docile. They come in a myriad of shapes, sizes, and colors. They're as varied as the colors of the rainbow. They get along with other fish just fine, which is why we see them mixed in with all kinds of other fish in aquariums. Everyone likes angelfish. They are fun to have around.

What I have found is that people can be like either puffer fish or angelfish. When we're acting like puffer fish, we blow ourselves up with pride to make ourselves look bigger than we are. We inflate our accomplishments. We become bloated about certain aspects of our personality. We try to make ourselves look bigger and better than those around us. And the toxins are released. It leaves a foul taste in the relational mouths of those around us. Sadly, the toxin of pride also repels God, who wants to give us his grace. When we act like puffer fish, most everyone gives us a wide berth.

When we act like angelfish, however, there's a natural draw. Others notice our unique beauty and distinctiveness—even from the other angelfish around us. With our natural, brilliant, God-given colors shining, people want to be around us. God desires to draw close as well. There's room for his glory and goodness when our sense of who we are is rightly shining.

Which better describes you, the puffer fish or the angelfish? How do you think God sees you?

The Subtlety of Pride

We need to be careful, though. At this point it's tempting to think, "Well, I'm obviously an angelfish. I mean, I'm not like the king in our story. I'm not some complete egomaniac that only pursues pleasure at all costs. I'm more humble than that. I think I have escaped the distance-producing hazard of pride."

What we need to recognize, however, is that pride can be subtle. It can creep in when we're feeling fine, and it can invade our souls when we least expect it. As my father was fond of saying when I was a kid, "There is a fine line between confidence and arrogance, and most people don't know when they've crossed it."

What I've noticed over the years, both in myself and in observing other believers, is that we can slip into pride unaware. Even as good-hearted followers of Jesus, we can become more like puffer fish than we realize. Maybe even *because* we're good-hearted followers. We feel good about all we're doing to live the Christian life. We feel good about our multifaceted attempts to live our side of the input-output equation described earlier on page 25. We feel good about our lives—especially compared to those around us. And though there's nothing wrong with feeling good about well-meaning attempts to follow Jesus, there's a fine line between feeling holy and feeling holier-than-thou.

Here are some signs that reveal that we may have crossed the thin line into pride:

- We find ourselves becoming judgmental of those who aren't doing as well as us.
- We find ourselves becoming unduly angry at the people around us when they don't share our values or live up to our expectations.
- We find ourselves feeling justified and satisfied with all our attempts to live out our faith. We may even feel like we've arrived.

- We find that those who know us well aren't as impressed with our well-honed spiritual strategies. They roll their eyes a bit at the duplicity they see.
- We find that though we might feel good about our attempts, we still feel far from God.

Any of these signs can and should serve as warning lights on the dashboard of your life telling you there could be something wrong under the hood.

A Daily Audit

One of the things I do each evening is what I call my *daily audit*. As I reflect on my day, I analyze two things: how I *related* to those around me and how I *thought* about the world around me. I audit my relationships and my attitude.

When it comes to each of my relational interactions for that day, I mentally go through the conversations and ask myself, "Was I a good listener? Did I say anything unkind or unfair? Did I try to lift myself up at their expense? Was I more like Jesus or more like the old Jamie?" In short, I audit my relationships to discern pride from humility.

Then I do the same with my attitude. "What did I think as I walked out of that stressful staff meeting? How did the news cycle affect my view of the world and culture around me? How well did I do on the freeway with my attitude toward other drivers?"

As you can imagine, there are plenty of times when my conscience is pricked, when God's Spirit speaks. I realize I said or thought something that was unfair and inappropriate toward another person. As I confess these shortcomings to the Lord,

I also make a mental note that I need to make amends. Occasionally, I will even jump up and send a quick email or text to the person I wounded by my pride. Most of the time the other person will say, "Oh, well . . . thanks. But it wasn't that big of a deal." But I know better. Though a small comment or seemingly benign thought might not seem like much in the grand scheme of things, added together and strung throughout one's days, weeks, months, and years they become the difference between a life built on pride and one built on humility. Our souls need to be kept in check. As I was taught years ago, we need to keep short accounts.

The daily audit is an introspective exercise I go through each evening. It's what the old-time spiritual writers refer to as managing one's interior life. It's not being afraid to take a look inside and being honest about what's there.

The writer of Proverbs beat us all to the punch with this when he wrote, "The purpose in a man's heart is like deep water, but a man of understanding will draw it out" (Prov. 20:5). For me, this daily audit allows me to monitor my purposes and draw them out on a consistent basis. It enables me to root out some of the hidden pride that's easy to gloss over in my heart and mind. And when I do this, I feel closer to God.

I encourage you to engage in a similar daily audit of your relational interactions and the thoughts that form your attitude. Whenever you choose to audit your relationships and thought life, it allows you to drive a wedge between distance-producing pride and closeness-producing humility.

The way of humility, though not a quick fix, gets you well on your way to feeling close to God once again. His grace is with us when we're humble. And his grace is meant to be felt and known.

WAY 3

Doing Right in the Right Way

Do the right thing. It will gratify some people and astonish the rest.

—Mark Twain

In the 1990s, when I pastored a church in the Midwest, there was a fellow in our congregation who, at least from the outside looking in, was unremarkable. Yet something he *did* made him a person who will always hold a special place in my life.

One day, as we were having lunch at a local restaurant, I asked this man what he did for a living. He told me he owned a small business in the then-burgeoning tech industry, casually mentioning it was his second company. He told me that tech start-ups can be risky and that he got in over his head financially with his first company. He had to shut it down and start over.

"But I still owe my creditors quite a substantial sum, and it will take me years to pay them," he said.

Having grown up in a business-minded family, I knew a little about corporations. So I asked why he hadn't filed under bankruptcy protection and been done with it. My friend said, "For me that was not an option. Most of my creditors are local, small-time merchants like me. I know them, and they know me. I promised to pay them for the credit and merchandise they extended me, and that's what I intend to do. As long as it takes."

I pastored in that area for almost a decade. When I eventually left, he was still paying what he owed. As far as I know, he paid every cent.

Over the years, I've met a few others who took a similar journey as my friend. They didn't feel that utilizing protection laws was in any way wrong—such laws exist for a reason, after all—but for them it was better to incur personal loss and pay what was promised. There's something unforgettable about this. There's something about going against the grain and doing what one sees as right—even at great personal cost—that draws me to these people.

Doing the right thing in the right way has everything to do with navigating times of divine distance.

The High Cost of Doing Right

The first two ways of navigating divine distance involve your inward state of being—your trust in God's providence and your character built on humility. Way 3 focuses more on what you *do* and how you *act*. Though costly and hard-won, choosing to do the right thing the right way will be indispensable in dealing with times when God feels far away.

We left off with Esther being chosen as queen and Mordecai wisely telling her to keep her Jewish faith hidden from the king. At that time, Jews in Persia were a conquered people. Deported from their homeland, they were at best second-class members of Persian society. At worst they were not members at all. They were tolerated but not completely trusted. Their faith in God and his commandments was not esteemed and respected. The ways of the Jewish people were foreign to the ways of the Persians. This created a conflict that becomes the heart of the book of Esther:

> After these things King Ahasuerus promoted Haman the Agagite, the son of Hammedatha, and advanced him and set his throne above all the officials who were with him. And all the king's servants who were at the king's gate bowed down and paid homage to Haman, for the king had so commanded concerning him. But Mordecai did not bow down or pay homage. (Esther 3:1–2)

As the antagonist in our story, Haman was clearly a puffer fish. In step with the king, he was consumed with himself, his own status, and his own power. Pride took center stage in his soul. Anger was the fuel that drove him, and whenever he was crossed, he responded with retribution. Haman's leadership formula of pride and vengeance wasn't a good combination. In Persian culture, bowing to another human being showed absolute submission and undying devotion. Bowing was a requirement whenever someone was in the presence of the king or a member of his inner circle.

For Mordecai, however, bowing was reserved only for God and never for any other human being. The first two commandments handed down to Moses couldn't be clearer: "You shall have no other gods before me. . . . You shall not *bow down* to them or serve them, for I the LORD your God am a jealous God" (Exod. 20:3, 5). Most scholars agree that mindfulness of these commands is what motivated Mordecai in his unwillingness to bow before Haman. Mordecai wasn't trying to be belligerent. He was following what was right as outlined by God in his Word. He was following God's law, even if it conflicted with human customs.

Mordecai's refusal to bow to Haman had serious, life-threatening repercussions for all the Jews living in Persia. Haman was incensed. His pride was wounded. And in accordance with his formula, his retribution was disproportionately severe:

> And when Haman saw that Mordecai did not bow down or pay homage to him, Haman was filled with fury. But he disdained to lay hands on Mordecai alone. So, as they had made known to him the people of Mordecai, Haman sought to destroy all the Jews, the people of Mordecai, throughout the whole kingdom of Ahasuerus. (Esther 3:5–6)

At that time, an estimated one million Jews lived in and around the vast Persian empire. This represented most Jews in the world. Because of what he perceived as disrespect from Mordecai, Haman plotted the complete annihilation of the Jewish people. All because of one man's single act of following God's law. The next sentence reveals Haman's plan: "In the first month, which is the month of Nisan, in the twelfth year of King Ahasuerus, they cast Pur (that is, they cast lots) before Haman day after day; and they cast it month after month till the twelfth month, which is the month of Adar" (3:7).

Being a superstitious culture, the ancient Persians made some decisions by rolling dice. *Purim* were simply Persian dice made from stones with markings on them. People at that time found direction based on certain ways the *purim* landed. As Haman rolled the dice, he determined the day set for exterminating the Jews.

Though the date was a few months away, it gave Haman time to mobilize the Persian people to commit genocide against the Jews. The rest of Esther 3 chronicles how Haman got the king to go along with his plan by convincing him that the Jews were opposed to Persian laws, which was not exactly true. He even paid the king for the right to carry out his plan. The king sealed the order with his signet ring—like we would sign a contract today—and the word was dispatched throughout Persia that the Jews would be destroyed.

If ever there was a high cost for doing right, this was it.

The Great Reversal

Mordecai's actions model a clear pathway in our own journey of following God when he feels distant. There's a temptation to think, "Why didn't Mordecai just bow? He wouldn't even have to mean it. God would have understood. It was life and death. It would have saved so much fear and grief, not just for him but for hundreds of thousands."

In looking closely at Mordecai's action, notice two things:

- Mordecai did what was right based on God's moral compass as found in his Word, the Jewish Scriptures.
- Mordecai did what was right regardless of the potential cost.

These two commitments were deeply rooted in the Jewish psyche. Going all the way back to Abraham, Jews were taught that when God tells you something is right, it's right. When God tells you to act, you act, whether it is to offer your son on the altar or to leave Egypt and head to the promised land or to stop whining in the desert or to go into battle and trust God that you will win. There are hundreds of scenarios in the Old Testament where God revealed his moral compass and expected his people to follow.

And though there might have been a cost to following, the cost was always worth it. How could it not be? They were following God. If they wanted to be close to him, they followed. They followed based on the moral compass he declared to them. And they did so regardless of the potential cost. What Mordecai was doing here was simply following the pattern all Jews had learned—a pattern that had served them well through thick and thin. In fact, it never went well for them when they broke the pattern—especially when it came to feeling close to the Lord.

Our modern culture has reversed this pattern. Today, many people do what they think is right based on the following two principles:

- Do what's right based on what I think is right in any given situation.
- Do what's right when it's convenient and beneficial.

Ethicists call this *situational ethics*. By abandoning any transcendent and absolute values that come down from on high (i.e., from God), this approach takes each situation in life as it comes and responds with what the individual personally feels is the right course to take. There's no set standard of values given to us by God. There's no written authority like the Bible to reveal what's right and wrong. The only thing that matters is what an individual personally *thinks* is right or wrong in any given situation, and they'll apply it when and how they want to. The result is that a person may choose what will most benefit themselves in any given situation. It doesn't have to always revolve around the self, but it opens the door wide for a more selfish orientation. Situational ethics lacks any outside help when it comes to moral direction, because its foundation is built solely on what one personally thinks and feels.

Please don't miss that this is a complete *reversal* of what we see in Mordecai's actions. His behavioral compass was set on God's true north as revealed in God's Word. This is how Mordecai chose to do what he did. Whether he *felt* like doing something wasn't his primary consideration. Even his own *thinking* was filtered through God's revelation in his law. What God wanted was what mattered to Mordecai, and it drove him in his actions. Though nobody intentionally pursues a bad outcome, the potential results or personal consequences were a secondary concern for Mordecai. What mattered was doing what was right in the eyes of God. Staying close to God depended on following God's moral compass.

I'd like to think that God's people are still following Mordecai's pattern today. However, after being a Christian for over forty years now—watching others and even auditing my own actions—there are too many times we opt for the world's reversal of Mordecai's way. Think of all the scenarios where we're tempted to compromise when it comes to our moral choices:

- Taxes: we cut corners.
- Truth telling: "It's just a white lie."

- Sexual ethics: "Waiting until marriage is so old-fashioned."
- Business ethics: "It's a dog-eat-dog world."
- Generosity: "Finances are always tight."
- Anger management: "I'm only human."

It's hard to walk the straight and narrow in today's increasingly immoral and secular culture. It's easy to fall into the great reversal.

Is It Worth It?

What we're noting in Esther's story is that *a significant part of navigating times when God feels far away is to maintain God's moral compass.*

Choosing his values even when the cost might be great. Doing the right thing in the right way. As Jesus said clearly and succinctly, "If you love me, you will keep my commandments" (John 14:15). Here we learn that *obedience matters.* And it matters most when you're navigating times of divine distance.

Far from a legalistic response to divine distance, where you simply live by a set of rules to somehow merit God's favor, there's an inherent logic to this way that is less about earning God's favor and more about protecting your soul. God's logic works to your advantage. Think about it: when God feels far away, you're more vulnerable to sin. You are spiritually dry. The tank is low. The motivation is waning. In those times, you might even be tempted to think, "Well, if God is going to be distant then I think I will return the favor." Right at this point, you are tempted to relax your guard. Apart from God, you're tempted to diverge from his moral compass. I can't even begin to tell you how many times I've witnessed good-hearted followers of Jesus—myself included—go down the low road. Most of us have stories of taking the moral low road when we felt spiritually weak.

God's logic continues. Responding to spiritual dryness with moral disregard doesn't help your cause in the least. In fact, it complicates it greatly. Think about it this way, if your child is feeling distant from you and responds with outright rebellion—not listening to anything you say and disregarding the house rules—does this foster closeness or further the distance? We all know the answer: it furthers the distance. Many households are rife with strife when a distant teenager decides to put aside the house rules. It's the same way in God's household.

> Doing right not only protects your soul from further feelings of distance but also offers you the best chance of seeing the light of day once again.

Ask yourself, "Is it worth maintaining my moral compass even when God feels far away?" The answer is obvious. Doing right not only protects your soul from further feelings of distance but also offers you the best chance of seeing the light of day once again. In fact, going back to the foundational way of trusting in the magnificent and unstoppable providence of God, maintaining your moral compass places you in the pathway of his good will. Even in light of the potential costs of doing right, bank on God's providence to not only see you through but also draw you close to him once again.

Mordecai, Esther, and the Jews experienced it. It can be your experience, too.

The Law of Rewards

The well-known Christian author Randy Alcorn leads a wonderful organization called Eternal Perspective Ministries. His mission is to teach people how to live each day with heaven in mind, as opposed to thinking only about the here and now. To accomplish this, Alcorn focuses on biblical education and social action. He believes that followers of Jesus should do right no matter the cost. Focusing on everything from racial reconciliation to world hunger to justice issues to pro-life advocacy, he has a consistent track record of following God's moral compass. As you can imagine, it's not been without cost. It's also not been without great blessing.

In his book *The Law of Rewards: Giving What You Can't Keep to Gain What You Can't Lose*, Alcorn tells a true story from 1989 when he served as a pastor in a suburb of Portland and also on the board of a pregnancy resource center. After praying to seek God's will about his role and looking for wisdom in the Scriptures, Alcorn decided to participate in nonviolent rescues at area abortion clinics. As a result of his actions, which included blocking access to the abortion clinics, Alcorn was arrested several times, and he spent a couple of nights in jail. He and other protesters were sued by the clinics, and the clinics were awarded a financial judgment. As a matter of conscience, Alcorn agreed to pay what he owed, but he refused to give money to any person or group that would use the funds to further their abortion practices. The government ultimately garnished 25 percent of his wages from the church to be paid to the abortion clinic. What happened next was Alcorn following Mordecai's way:

> The church would either have to pay the abortion clinic or defy a court order. To avoid this, I had to resign. The only way I could prevent garnishment in the future was to make no more than minimum wage. Another court judgment followed, involving another abortion clinic. We were assessed the largest judgment ever against a group of peaceful protesters: $8.2 million. By all appearances, our lives had taken a devastating turn.[1]

Because abortion is a highly combustible issue in today's culture, Alcorn's reputation in the eyes of many was shot. Like Mordecai, one act of righteousness—based clearly on God's moral compass as outlined in his Word—brought devastating repercussions. The court assessment against Alcorn went on for two decades, and he did not return to local church ministry. Instead, he started a nonprofit ministry where he never earns more than minimum wage. In the state of Oregon, minimum wage is not subject to court garnishment, so the plaintiffs never received any money from the church where he had served nor from him. Randy's wife worked as a secretary and provided for their family for twenty years. To keep the family's income at the minimum-wage level, they decided that Eternal Perspective Ministries would own any and all books Randy would write and that the proceeds would go to needed charities.

God is sovereign, however. His providence is worthy of our trust. And doing right is always the right thing. You see, poverty and defeat were not the end of the story for Alcorn—not by a long shot.

Then something interesting happened: suddenly my books were on the bestseller lists. Royalties increased. Our ministry has been able to give away 100 percent of those royalties to missions, famine relief, and pro-life work. . . . Sometimes I think God sells the books just to raise funds for ministries close to his heart! I don't go to bed at night feeling that I've "sacrificed" that money, wishing somehow I could get my hands on it. I go to bed feeling joy.[2]

Don't miss that last word: *joy*. I'm reminded of the psalmist's experience when he wrote, "Weeping may tarry for the night, but joy comes with the morning" (Ps. 30:5). Though the high cost of doing right hurts for a while, God is always good for a jolt of joy with the morning.

And sometimes the joy is overwhelming. When Alcorn included this story in his book it was 2003. In a July 2019 update on his website, he shared that since the time of the original judgment against him, his books have produced a revenue of over $8.2 million. Almost the same amount as the original assessment against him. And true to their word, Alcorn and his ministry have given it all away to needy causes that promote societal healing and spiritual health.[3]

I love how Alcorn summarized the last three decades of his up-and-down spiritual journey:

See how God continues to use me going to jail and losing my job as a pastor and those lawsuits . . . to further His Kingdom? . . . It brings a big smile to my face. . . . We thank our sovereign God for bringing us such freedom and joy in a way we never saw coming and never would have chosen, but which—if we had it to do over again—would do nothing to change.[4]

I've heard quite a few of God's people say similar things to that over the years. Though the journey can be very difficult at times—especially when we take the road less traveled and do what is right and true—when we look back at how our sovereign God used it, we would change nothing. Mordecai would agree.

It Feels Like God

Years ago, I served at a church where our senior pastor was a man who *felt* very deeply. He didn't simply feel strongly *about* things, he felt deeply *in* and *with* most all things in life. On the famous Myers-Briggs temperament scale, he was a strong "feeler" as opposed to a "thinker." This didn't mean he was not bright or intelligent—he was both. It meant that he couldn't decide without filtering it through his emotions first. When we were making decisions as a staff team, it wasn't uncommon for him to say, "That feels like God to me," or conversely, "That doesn't feel like God to me." He would literally make decisions based on whether something *felt* like God or not. As a strong thinker myself, I can remember pondering, "What precisely does God *feel* like?" The idea of basing a decision on what God might or might not feel like didn't compute to me back then.

I've grown and matured over the years, but I still don't base my decisions primarily on what feels like God. My temperament is more rational than visceral. That said, I do relate with something "feeling like God" more today than I did in my youth. When I feel far from God and yet obediently follow his moral compass, it feels better. I feel that he's smiling on me and proud of me for remaining true to his directives. And, over time, I eventually feel closer to him as a result. Doing right in the right way helps me navigate divine distance.

Think of all the ethical situations you face today. Now add spiritual dryness and confusion into the mix. You get the picture. You're in a vulnerable place. Imagine, however, what the picture looks like when you follow Mordecai's way of doing right in the right way. You still might be confused and dry at first, but as you engage in obedience to God's Word and combine it with the fortitude that moves forward despite the cost, you will have a recipe for navigating divine distance. You'll keep your integrity even when things seem dim or dark. And you very well may know what it's like to feel God.

Doing right in the right way is a proven pathway to navigating divine distance.

Even though God might feel far away from you at this time, he loves you. He's in complete control of your chaos. So keep following his moral compass and choose what is right. He might feel distant now, but as you walk the narrow path, he will draw you close once again. And joy will come in the morning.

WAY 4

Making Good Decisions in the Storm

Decision is the spark that ignites action.

—Wilfred A. Peterson

Though it happened more than twenty years ago, I remember the experience like it happened just yesterday. I was two years into pastoring a struggling, come-back church in the Midwest. It was an uphill climb, but things were going well. The church was growing. God's people were getting a second wind. Lost people were placing their faith in Jesus. The changes we made were finally paying off. The leadership and staff were in harness with one another. And I was tired.

That spring, I decided to take a study break at my parents' condo in Jackson Hole, Wyoming. It was an idyllic place to try to reconnect with God and prepare for some upcoming sermons. It was just me and God as I spent two weeks by myself with an open Bible, a few commentaries, and the Grand Tetons as the backdrop.

For reasons I can't explain to this day, I felt very dry spiritually and far from God. I had been feeling this way for a few months, which seemed like an eternity. Don't get me wrong. I was reading the Bible regularly, confessing my shortcomings to the Lord daily, and talking to him a lot. There was no unconfessed, unchecked sin in my life that might block his felt presence. I was in loving relationship with my wife and kids, and I was even in a weekly men's accountability group. In terms of the input-output equation, I was doing everything I knew (and had been taught) to stay close to God.

But for reasons unknown, I felt he was, at best, behind the scenes of my daily life. And it wasn't simply due to fatigue, either. There are plenty of times when I feel tired in ministry and still feel close to God. I call those times a "good tired."

This was different. Despite doing all I knew to stay close to the Lord, it wasn't working like it had in the past, and I didn't have a good explanation why.

While on this study break, I got a phone call that complicated matters greatly. The call didn't originate from my current church but was from a man at my home church back in Ohio. This was the church I attended when I first became a Christian back in the early 1980s. It was the church that baptized me and helped me grow in my new faith and where I had done a summer internship during seminary. It was the church where Kim and I got married and where we dedicated one of my children to the Lord.

The man on the phone was head of the search team tasked with finding a replacement for the church's retiring senior pastor, who had founded the church and had been there for twenty-five years. He was a friend and mentor to me. The search team was doing a nationwide search, and they had narrowed it down to five candidates. Due to my rich history with the church, they wanted to add my name to the short list. "Would you be interested?" the man asked.

The prospect of pastoring my home church was a dream come true. I wanted to jump at the chance. Yet my current church still needed me. I wanted to know what God wanted for all involved. I wanted his will, not simply mine. The real crux of the matter, however, was making a life-altering, spiritual decision when I didn't feel spiritually strong. I remember thinking, "How can I make a decision like this when I'm trying to navigate divine distance? It's difficult enough to make tough calls in line with God's will when the waters are calm. How do I make a decision like this in the storm?"

The Triple Threat

I was in a tough spot. I was experiencing what I have come to call "the triple threat." It occurs when three things collide:

- A tough decision confronts us
- We want to make the decision in line with God's will
- But we are not in a good place spiritually to discern his will

In these scenarios, time is of the essence. We don't have the luxury of waiting. The storm is raging around us, but we still need to navigate the boats of our lives to shore. The shore can't be seen. The GPS is acting up. It's too risky to wait out the storm. We need to get moving. How do we navigate in the storm?

My guess is that many, if not most, of us can relate to this triple threat. You have a tough call to make. It might involve your work, your marriage, or your kids. It might involve an important relationship. It might have to do with a business or financial decision. Or, like me twenty years ago, it might have to do with a significant move, perhaps even something involving church. A significant decision needs to be made, and it can't wait.

Being tenderhearted toward God, you want to make this decision in line with his will. You want to know what God thinks. You want to be sensitive to the leading of his Spirit. You want to stay in the lane of his direction for your life. You don't want to take matters into your own hands and risk a bad decision that might take years to undo. You want what God wants.

But there is a third part of this triple threat that complicates it all: you feel far from God. It's not like you have strayed—you could fix that easily. All you'd have to do is stop straying and turn back to God (the Bible calls this repentance). No, you're doing all you know to stay close. You don't feel that you've wandered. Nevertheless, you feel a distance. Prayers don't breed the intimacy with God that they once did. Bible reading is not as crisp and sharp. Fellowship and service are duties and chores more than soul-enhancing experiences. To borrow the image from our story in Esther, you feel like you're an exile in a strange land—not quite at home in your spiritual life and not quite in that sweet spot with God.

It's the triple threat. It's when we realize that navigating divine distance isn't just about doing the right thing but also making the right decisions. When you are making a tough call, how does that work?

Nothing New under the Sun

It might comfort you to know that Esther and her people experienced this triple threat. It's an age-old dilemma. It will be especially helpful to see how they handled it during the times when God felt far away.

Soon after Mordecai's God-honoring, costly choice to not bow to Haman, the news of Haman's plan to destroy all the Jews in Persia became widely known. The king went along with the plan, unaware that his new queen was Jewish, and he believed Haman's story that the Jews were a rebellious, law-breaking people. There was also a bribe involved (money tends to be a great motivation in this fallen world). As you can imagine, the Jews were wrecked. Tremendous fear gripped them.

Mordecai has a plan, however. Through an emissary, he delivers word of Haman's plot to Queen Esther. He relays all the details: his refusal to bow, Haman's anger-management problems, the lies to the king, and the rolling of the dice (*purim*) to pick a day to destroy the Jews. He even provides proof in the written decrees sent out by Haman and the king. It's an airtight case. He instructs Esther to go to her husband, explain what's been happening, and "beg his favor and plead with him on behalf of [our] people" (Esther 4:8).

But for Esther it isn't so easy. Her response to Mordecai shows why:

> All the king's servants and the people of the king's provinces know that if any man or woman goes to the king inside the inner court without being called, there is but one law—to be put to death, except the one to whom the king holds out the golden scepter so that he may live. But as for me, I have not been called to come in to the king these thirty days. (4:11)

85

What a crazy culture! This king whom Esther was married to had a rule that if anyone (even the queen) entered into his inner court (where decisions were made for the kingdom) without his personal summons, they would be killed. The only exception was if the king chose to have compassion that day and extend the golden scepter as a sign of his benevolent kindness and patience. And the petitioner wouldn't know until it was too late. Basically, Esther says to Mordecai, "My husband is consumed with power and driven by anger. If I go barging in to plead for our people, even though he likes me at times and has a soft spot for me, it could be the death of me and not much hope for our people."

Esther was experiencing the triple threat. A tough call needed to be made: risk her life and go see the king without being summoned. She wanted to make this decision as a Jew—a follower of God—using his wisdom and values. But she was all alone and felt spiritually anemic. She and her people were in exile. There was no temple, no reading of the covenant or law, no priests performing sacrifices, and few words from God through the prophets. Everything they had known and been accustomed to when it came to connecting with God was missing. God was there, and they knew it, but he was behind the scenes.

> When God feels far away, **self-denial** and **other-centeredness** are well-worn pathways toward making the right call.

Like Esther, millions of God's people down through the centuries have experienced their own triple threats in life. A difficult decision needs to be made that cannot wait. There is a desire to make the decision according to God's will and purposes. Spiritual remoteness complicates the process. It's the perfect storm.

Making a Good Decision in the Storm

So how do we do this? How do we make decisions at the crossroads, especially when God seems distant and our spiritual tank is low?

The answer has everything to do with navigating divine distance. It's an answer that I don't hear often or read about in books on how to discern God's will. Yet it's thoroughly biblical, and it not only provides a workable pathway for making a good and godly decision but it also helps us draw close to the Lord along the way.

When we look closely at the pattern set forth by Esther, we observe this principle at work: when God feels far away, *self-denial* and *other-centeredness* are well-worn pathways toward making the right call.

In light of the triple threat and Esther's understandable ambivalence about going to the king, Mordecai replies,

> Do not think to yourself that in the king's palace you will escape any more than all the other Jews. For if you keep silent at this time, relief and deliverance will rise for the Jews from another place, but you and your father's house will perish. And who knows whether you have not come to the kingdom for such a time as this? (Esther 4:13–14)

Mordecai issues a twofold challenge: He first tells Esther, "Do not think to yourself." In other words, "Don't just make this about what's easy for you, but dig deep and deny your own selfish impulses." He wants her to deny the fear that is tempting her toward self-protection.

The reason is seen in Mordecai's second challenge: "Think of your fellow Jews. Become other-centered. Realize that God will deliver them one way or the other, but the best way is for him to use you! Take a risk and act."

Based on this twofold challenge of self-denial and other-centeredness, Esther utters three words that change history: "I will go" (4:16).

We don't want to miss the profundity of Mordecai's spiritual and psychological challenge to Esther. The core of his logic is that while going to the king involves a significant risk (banishment or even death), the decision isn't all that difficult. If it could save Israel and give life to others, then it is the right and godly decision. That's what being selfless and focused on others is all about. It's God's way. Plowing right through the spiritual confusion and divine distance she feels, Esther makes a good decision—a great one really. One that will save her people and draw those involved close to God once again. Self-denial and other-centeredness—this was Mordecai's recipe.

Don't think for a minute that Mordecai was somehow being insensitive or unempathetic toward Esther. He loved Esther deeply. He had raised her as his own. He checked on her daily at the palace gate. She was like a daughter to him. Mordecai knew the risks involved and that his counsel to Esther could mean her death.

He also knew something else: when God feels far away, self-denial and other-centeredness are his well-worn pathways toward making the right call. It's a truism about life this side of heaven. It's a key principle for living in times when God feels far away. It's vital to making a good decision in the storm.

God's Reverse Economics for Decision-Making

Most of us are familiar with how modern economics works. It follows this formula:

$$\text{Cost to others} + \text{Benefit to you} = \text{Success}$$

In other words, success happens when you can find or make a way for other people to bear and pay a cost that directly benefits you. It's Economics 101, built upon supply and demand. If you want to be successful in the economic realm, develop a product that others desire or need and get them to buy it (or pay the cost) so that you will benefit (i.e., make a profit). When this happens, you're on your way to success. That's how most successful businesspeople make money. It's our world's system of economics. And though it's not bad or wrong (it's how we make a living, after all), it's problematic when we make this the sum total of how we live. In other words, we shouldn't drag this formula from our vocational and economic world into our personal and spiritual world.

Sadly, I see this happen often. People approach their relationships (marriage, kids, friendships, etc.), their church, their community, their personal lives, and even their walk with God with the same economic formula we find in culture. When marriage gets tricky and stops benefiting us, it's no longer successful and it's time to get out. When conflict with a friend propels us into the infamous tunnel of chaos and the cost becomes too high, maybe it's time to throw in the towel. When the battle with sin is difficult and the cost is too high, we just give in. When it's too hard to keep the anger at bay, we let it fly.

We treat our spiritual and personal lives like a business transaction. If it costs too much and benefits others more than self, then the bottom line doesn't work anymore.

It's time to recalculate the equation. When it comes to making right choices during times of divine distance, it's fascinating and instructive to see how God *reverses* this formula:

$$\text{Cost to you} + \text{Benefit to others} = \text{Right choice}$$

It's the *opposite* of our world's system of success. It's *reverse economics*, an upending of how our world tells us to live. God says, "If you want to make decisions and choices that bring me honor, advance my kingdom, model what my Son was all about, and bring you ultimate joy and peace, then make choices that benefit *others* and cost *you* something." Jesus said for a person to find their life, they must lose it.[1] For those who want to be successful in the spiritual and relational realms, they must love others just as much (or even more) than they love themselves.

A Tough Call Made

Years ago, when I was out in Wyoming struggling with the triple threat, I made a decision. I decided to leave my pastoral post in Canada and go to my home church in the Cleveland area. What tilted me toward this decision, even in the midst of spiritual dryness, were the twin values of self-denial and other-centeredness. Sure, I wanted to go and pastor my home church. It was very much the desire of my heart. Yet, putting this aside, as I sought wise counsel and thought about it reasonably, I realized that my home church needed me, and I was the best choice for them. A church is vulnerable when a founding pastor of twenty-five years retires. Many times, the new leader doesn't make it more than a year or two and becomes a sacrificial lamb. It helps if the new person is a known commodity and someone who has the right skills to lead through a transition. As I thought about it (as clearly as I could) and prayed about it (though prayers at that time seemed to bounce off the spiritual atmosphere), I saw that I had spent the previous twelve years of pastoral ministry helping two churches through rugged transitions. If anything, I *was* a transition leader. I knew some of the pitfalls as well as the proven strategies that could help my home church move into its next season of productive ministry. This would all take an immense amount of trust. My history with my home church already had a built-in trust factor. We could hit the ground running and begin a new season of ministry.

As they say, hindsight is always 20/20. Five years after my arrival there, my home church had doubled in size, hundreds of lost people had come home to Jesus, and very few of the original congregation had left during the seasons of transition and growth that followed. Though going back to my home church was every bit as difficult as any work I had done before, it proved to be a good decision. Even better, the season of spiritual dryness that originally led me to Wyoming eventually passed. The spiritual sun shone once again. And I realized that making the decision I did was actually a part of the good spiritual weather. It helped lift the cloud cover and draw me close to God once again. It helped me navigate my season of divine distance.

Consider This . . .

Think about what your life would look like if you applied Mordecai's counsel when you're facing the triple threat. What would your life look like if you approached your tough call with a cost-to-you plus benefit-to-others response? How might this affect your marital frustration? Your wayward kid? Your neighbor who drives you crazy? The sin that continually grips you? The difficult decision to go this way or that? Consider how different your life and decisions might look beneath Mordecai's twofold challenge.

Then consider further how this might affect times when God feels far away. Making good and godly decisions must have some impact on this, don't you think? It certainly did for Esther and her people. Her amazing choice not only delivered her people from a very real and life-destroying threat but was the catalyst for drawing them close to God once again. Spoiler alert: the story has a happy ending with a huge party that Jews around the world still celebrate today. And it all stemmed from Esther's single decision. A good decision made in the storm. It's how we navigate divine distance.

WAY 5

Creating God Room in Your Life

A miracle is when the whole is greater than the sum of its parts. A miracle is when one plus one equals a thousand.

—Frederick Buechner

Sometimes the simplest concepts are the most profound. "A penny saved is a penny earned." "The early bird catches the worm." "No pain, no gain." We all relate to these simple phrases. They communicate something rich about saving, working, and getting ahead. I want to introduce you to another simple but profound concept—one that will have everything to do with navigating divine distance. It's the concept of *God room.*

God Room

I first learned about God room from Franklin Graham, the eldest son of the famous evangelist Billy Graham. He assumed leadership of his dad's ministry as Billy advanced into his later years of life. Long before that, though, Franklin wrote an auto-biography where he shared what it was like growing up as the son (and living in the tall shadow) of such a famous Christian man. Writing about his younger years spent rebelling against God and family and of his eventual return to faith in Jesus, Franklin titled his book *Rebel with a Cause: Finally Comfortable Being Graham.*

The book includes the stirring story of Franklin's departure from and return to faith that resulted in his assuming leadership of the international relief ministry Samaritan's Purse. In the book, Graham tells the story of Samaritan's Purse founder Bob Pierce, a man who mentored the returning prodigal. Bob wasn't who you might expect to be used for this purpose; he was an unlikely candidate, because he had faced several of his own significant challenges over the years: a troubled marriage, professional struggles (including founding and eventually losing an international ministry organization), mental health issues, and a daughter's suicide. Any one of these could completely derail a person. All of them together are almost too much to bear! Somehow, Bob persevered, compelled by a deeply rooted desire to see people come to faith in God through trusting in Jesus as their Lord and Savior.

In 1975, Bob took Franklin on a whirlwind trip to some of the neediest parts of the world: Korea, Hong Kong, China, India, Iran, and remote jungle villages in Thailand. The goal was to have Franklin see the crying need the world has for physical relief and the gospel of Jesus. In a key moment in the trip, while immersed deep within the jungle, Bob shared a central aspect of his faith and trust in God. Graham describes it this way:

The lesson Bob taught me that stands out above all the rest is what Bob called "God room." . . . [As Bob put it,] "God room" is when you see a need and it's bigger than your human abilities to meet it. But you accept the challenge. You trust God to bring in the [resources] to meet the need.[1]

Later that trip, to make sure Franklin truly understood, Bob restated the principle even more plainly:

God room is when you have seen a need you believe God wants you to meet. You try, but you can't. After you've exhausted all your human effort, there's still a gap. No matter what you do, you just can't humanly bring it about. That's when you pray and leave room for God to work. You watch God close the gap.[2]

God room. Creating space in your decisions and actions where you're leaving room for God to fill and do the things that only he can do. Faith is explained in the Bible as "the assurance of things hoped for, the conviction of things not seen" (Heb. 11:1). In a sense, creating God room is just a matter of living by faith where you're trusting God more than yourself and your ingenuity. It's intentionally looking for and expecting his movement, his activity, and his timing when all your human effort is exhausted and abandoned. It's understanding that you can do what God will have you do, but there's a part of your life's circumstances where if God does not move and act then it won't happen. And so you make space—room—for God to move and act.

Creating God room is what makes the difference between what I've heard Larry Crabb refer to as *naturally* accessible reality and *supernaturally* accessible reality. It's giving God the space to enter into your life and move in such a way that diminishes the divine distance you might feel.

Esther's Problem

Esther faced a difficult dilemma. Her people were being threatened with genocide, and she was uniquely able to do something about it by going to her husband, the king, and trying to get him to reverse his own decree. Though he was an irrational leader, driven by anger and emotion, he had a soft spot for his new bride, and if she caught him in a good mood, he just might relent. Remember, too, that the king was unaware of Esther's Jewish heritage. Arming him with that information could turn the tide for her and her people. Esther needed to go in and plead her case.

But not so fast. There were crazy rules in this ancient Middle Eastern culture. If a person, even the queen, sought a formal audience with the king without being summoned, death was the penalty. The only exception was if the king decided to allow it in the moment by extending his golden scepter as a sign of his good will and willingness to listen. This was Esther's best shot at exposing Haman's plan to exterminate the Jews in Persia. She had to seek a formal audience with the king and plead her case.

So how should Esther have proceeded? What would you do, faced with the same situation? What's the plan? What now?

We come to the dramatic moment in the story when we see Esther create God room, that space where God does the works that are far too big for any person to accomplish. It is in this place that God gives Esther the vision of how to proceed. In fact, one of the most fascinating things in all of Scripture happens here: God reveals to Esther the steps she must take in the daring plan to save her fellow Jews. This plan was impossible by human standards. It was something she never could have pulled off on her own as a powerless immigrant bride of a power-crazy, egotistical king. This plan involved *three distinct phases*, with each phase designed to make even more God room. Each phase would *create space*—space for God to show up and do what only he could do. Let's explore together these phases and notice the brilliance of Esther's well-laid plan.

Phase 1: The Setup

After Esther agreed to approach the king—and after three days of fasting and giving God plenty of space to move and act—Esther is found waiting outside the king's inner court. We can picture her in a holding pattern, waiting for something to happen to move things along. The king noticed her. He invited her in. He extended the golden scepter, which meant he was open to hearing what she had to say.

Then the king said to her, "What is troubling you, Queen Esther? And what is your request? Even to half of the kingdom it shall be given to you" (Esther 5:3 NASB).

Imagine if you were Esther at this point: you had just gotten past the major hurdle of winning an audience with the king, and not only did he *not* kill you for your unannounced visit, but he was so happy to see you that he offered you up to *half his kingdom*—a territory that was about the size of the southern half of the United States. What would you do now?

Most of us would think, "This is definitely an open door given to me by God. Now is the time to ask the king what I came here to ask!" We'd go ahead and ask away. We've all had the experience of reading the room or feeling out the mood of a spouse, a parent, or a boss before making a big request. Typically, when we get a sense of a good mood or that we're in good graces, we go for it.

Esther doesn't do that. Instead, she responds, "If it pleases the king, may the king and Haman come this day to the banquet that I have prepared for him" (Esther 5:4 NASB).

In response to the king's favorable mood toward her, she makes no mention of her request. She doesn't drop the bomb, shoot up a warning flare, or capitalize on Ahasuerus's good mood. Instead of going for it and making her request, she invites the king and Haman to dinner. It doesn't make sense. What is Esther doing? As crazy as it seems, it's all part of the plan to allow for more God room—a plan designed to create space for God to do what only he can do. On the heels of this setup phase, Esther is now ready to embark on the next phase of her well-laid plan.

Phase 2: Create Some Room

> Then the king said, "Bring Haman quickly that we may do as Esther desires." So the king and Haman came to the banquet that Esther had prepared. As they drank their wine at the banquet, the king said to Esther, "What is your petition, for it shall be granted to you. And what is your request? Even to half of the kingdom it shall be done." (Esther 5:5–6 NASB)

You might be thinking, "Okay, now is the time for Esther to go for the jugular and convince the king to prevent the slaughter of the Jews." After a sumptuous feast and a little wine, while the king is still in a generous mood, this seems like the opportune moment to act.

Most of us would choose to make our move right at this moment, because that's how we typically operate in our own experiences. We are able to recognize the signs when a person is primed and ready to give us whatever we may be after. We've been to a Tony Robbins seminar or we've read the Zig Ziglar books. We listen to the latest leadership podcasts that have modernized and updated Dale Carnegie's timeless techniques. Most of us are decent at navigating our relationships with discernment and have developed a keen sense of when to hold back and when to play the cards we've been dealt.

Esther, though, hadn't been to Robbins's seminars. She couldn't benefit from any of Ziglar's books, which had yet to be written. She wasn't exposed to techniques on how to win friends and influence people. She was a foreign woman with virtually no rights, and she was placing herself and the entire Jewish population at tremendous risk if this didn't work.

But Esther had a plan. A plan to allow Providence to win the day. A plan to allow some room for God to move. So she moved on to a further and final phase that would change everything, one that would accomplish much more than her human ingenuity ever could.

Phase 3: Create Even More Room

> So Esther replied, "My petition and my request is: if I have found favor in the sight of the king, and if it pleases the king to grant my petition and do what I request, may the king and Haman come to the banquet which I will prepare for them, and tomorrow I will do as the king says." (Esther 5:7–8 NASB)

For most of us reading Esther's story, this is confusing and yet at the same time captivating. What is she doing? A casual reader might wrestle with trying to understand why Esther developed and executed this staggered, stalling, and outright maze-like plan to get Ahasuerus to see Haman's plot to kill the Jews. For thousands of years, different Bible experts have likewise struggled to make sense of her plan. They have suggested everything from fear (causing her to move slowly), to psychological manipulation (delay tactics formulated to soften the king), to saying that's just how culture was back then (taking one's time to get to the point), to "author inclusion" (these scenes were added by the author to spice things up, but they never really happened). The problem with all these explanations is that they are either historically untenable or they don't seem to make the best sense of what is happening.

> **Esther developed plans that created space for God to enter into and fill. In creating this space, she expected that Providence would smile upon her and her people.**

No, something else altogether must be running through Esther's mind. As we have been noting all along, Esther's actions implicitly demonstrate *faith*. Esther operates with a sense that God is behind the scenes in all that is happening. Given this context, I believe Esther is taking a deliberate approach that slows the momentum. She moves at an even and concerted pace to allow plenty of room for God's intervention. As the Jewish people fast and wait, Esther's actions intentionally leave space for God to move. Her pace gives room for God to uniquely act and breathe life into her plans. Her process affords God a place to show up and do whatever he will choose to deliver his people.

This understanding of the passage explains Esther's start and stop approach. She moved forward during phase 1 when she first approached the king and then *stopped*. She moved forward some more during phase 2 and again *stopped*. She then moved forward further during phase 3 and *stopped* a third time. Each time, she simply advanced and paused, waiting and giving God ample room to orchestrate everything necessary in answer to her and her people's prayers. Given that faith in God's providence is such a major theme throughout the book of Esther, this understanding makes the most sense of her actions. Esther developed plans that created space for God to enter into and fill. In creating this space, she expected that Providence would smile upon her and her people.

The Result of Creating Space

What happens between the first and second banquet occurs in such a way that even the most skeptical mind would have to chalk it up to some kind of divine intervention.

Here are the seemingly coincidental events that take place in the space Esther created:

- Haman, the enemy of the Jews, bumps into Mordecai and remembers how much he resented him for not bowing and showing submission.
- As a prelude to genocide, Haman decides to hang Mordecai the very next day and has a gallows built.
- That night, the king has a bout of insomnia and asks to have a history book read aloud to make him sleepy.

- The story chosen by the king's servant is the account of how Mordecai had foiled a plot to assassinate the king—loyalty that had never been rewarded.
- The next morning, the king asks Haman to advise him on the best way to honor a person for their loyalty, but he doesn't tell Haman the person is Mordecai.
- Haman, thinking that the king must want to honor him, suggests a parade through the city so that all could see the man whom the king wants to honor.
- The king loves the idea, and only then does he reveal that the one being honored is Mordecai. He also designates Haman to lead Mordecai on his parade through the city.
- Haman is humiliated as the king honors the man he had planned to hang from the gallows!

Don't forget that all this happens in the interlude between the two banquets. Not until the second banquet would Esther reveal Haman's plan to annihilate the Jewish people—including Mordecai, the man whom the king honors before the entire city, and Queen Esther, whom the king adores.

Look again at the list above. While any one of these events might not be unusual—particularly such common occurrences as meeting one's enemy in town or battling a case of insomnia—the likelihood of all these things happening *together* is incredibly small. The odds of them all happening in this exact sequence and time frame is a statistical impossibility. Even the most skeptical minds have to marvel at the coincidence. With hindsight illumined by an informed faith, we can see God's hand behind the scenes breaking through and intervening in the affairs of these people.

There's no way that Esther could have orchestrated all this herself. Only God could do this. Only God could work behind the scenes and order events so perfectly. Esther simply slowed down enough to leave plenty of room for God to move amidst the details of her circumstances. Neil Breneman, an expert on the story of Esther, agrees: "Esther sensed that the time was not right for her important request. Time was needed for some other details to fall into place—in God's providence—before Esther made her request."[3]

How to Create God Room

God room is something every one of us could use in our lives. In fact, it's something that each of us needs more of in our fast-paced, well-intentioned, mistake-riddled lives. The challenge with God room is common to every one of us: God room is a lot easier to talk about than it is to actually make room for in our lives.

The key to creating God room is *waiting*—a concept that most of us either have little experience with or simply don't want to hear about. In this case, we must *wait on God*. It's not easy. Waiting goes against the grain of our modern culture. We live in a world that screams to us on a regular basis and with a sense of urgency, "Don't just stand there—do something!" When crisis hits our lives, urgency increases even more, and the call gets even louder.

God, however, operates differently. In response to times of chaos in our lives, God quietly instructs us, "Don't just do something—stand there." God says, "Look to me. Wait for me. Give me room in your plans to do what only I can do for you."

It's a foreign concept to twenty-first-century ears, but waiting is something we see throughout the Bible. God's people had been waiting on God for thousands of years. Long before Esther found herself waiting on God between two dinner parties, Moses led the people of Israel out of bondage to Egypt, and he experienced times of waiting in crisis after crisis. One dramatic moment was when Moses and all Israel were camped on the shore of the Red Sea as Pharaoh's murderous army stormed toward them in chariots. As the army drew near, the people panicked and cried out to the Lord. Logic and common sense screamed, "Fight, flee, or surrender!" Instead, Moses waited on God. He created God room, offering the people a supernatural alternative that required them *not* to act but simply to stand:

> But Moses said to the people, "Do not fear! Stand by and see the salvation of the LORD which He will accomplish for you today; for the Egyptians whom you have seen today, you will never see them again forever. The LORD will fight for you while you keep silent." (Exod. 14:13–14 NASB)

When Moses created space and waited on God, God supernaturally protected Israel, putting literal space between them and Pharaoh's army. As God had instructed him, Moses then stretched his hand over the sea, and God parted the waters to make a way where there had before not been a way.

God room is found only when we learn to wait on God.

God room is found only when we learn to wait on God. It's what Esther did. Like Esther, we need to leave plenty of God room in our own plans and decisions—room that honors God's activity and accounts for his timing. It's central to navigating times of divine distance. We want to see God again. We want to sense his movement in our lives. This happens when we slow down our own plans enough to allow for God to move and accomplish his work in his time. It's what many of us need to do. Creating God room is core to navigating times when God feels far away. So exactly *how* do we do this? What's involved in learning to wait on God with the goal of seeing his movement once again in our lives?

Waiting on God

For many people, the very idea of waiting on God is difficult to wrap our brains around. Even if we understand the idea, we find it even more difficult to wrap our hands around. Our attempts at waiting on God end up looking far different from what is portrayed in the Bible. Typically, waiting on God might feel like when a wife tells her husband, "Give me ten minutes to finish dressing for the dinner party, and then we can go." Or when a husband tells his wife, "There are only five minutes left in the game. I'll clean the garage in five minutes." In both scenarios, waiting is relatively short-lived but it's not a very positive experience.

The Bible's portrayal of waiting on God is much more positive and life-giving. It prepares us for the long haul with God. When waiting on God becomes a natural part of our ongoing faith journey, it produces incredible benefits such as creating God room. Waiting is how we navigate times of divine distance and draw close to God once again.

As I mentioned at the beginning of this chapter, we need to look closely at this section of Esther's story to get the most out of it and discover the secret to creating God room. In this vein, let's wrap up the chapter by looking closely at how Esther waits on God. She'll show us how to wait until we see the light of day once again. There are at least three tools Esther utilizes within her waiting that make all the difference.

Wait Expectantly

> Now it came about on the third day that Esther put on her royal robes and stood in the inner court of the king's palace in front of the king's rooms, and the king was sitting on his royal throne in the throne room, opposite the entrance to the palace. (Esther 5:1 NASB)

Notice that Esther sets herself up in view of her husband, the king. She stands (waiting) in the inner court for an indefinite period of time, hoping the king will notice her and invite her in. She waits *expectantly*—leaving lots of God room—hoping as she does so that God will intervene and cause the king to look kindly upon her.

It doesn't end there. We can picture Esther waiting expectantly throughout each stage of her well-laid plan. Between each phase, we can picture her advancing, stalling, hoping, and waiting with anticipation, leaving room for God to intervene and do something that will cause a turn of events to favor her and her people. Just like I waited for my then-girlfriend, Kim, to arrive for one of our rare in-person visits during our time of long-distance dating, glancing out the window every now and then to see if her car was coming down the road, Esther eagerly watches for Providence to come through for her and her people. Waiting expectantly keeps our eyes clearly focused on the horizon, looking and hoping for God to reveal himself in whatever way he chooses.

Waiting expectantly is what sets faith-illed, hope-filled followers of God apart from the sad-sack, pessimistic, doom-and-gloom people we all know. Waiting on God isn't designed to be a depressing, miserable, gloomy, dismal experience. It's not even meant to be arduous or difficult, though it does take patience. Waiting on God is meant to be the kind of experience in which you wait with great anticipation, eagerly looking to experience God and what he's going to do next.

> Waiting on God is meant to be the kind of experience in which you wait with great anticipation, eagerly looking to experience God and what he's going to do next.

Sure enough, the God who is behind the scenes does in fact intervene for Esther and her people and brings about the deliverance that only he can. More than simply having the king show favor to Esther and the Jewish people, the result will get their enemy, Haman, out of the way and pave the way for the Jews to defend themselves and find justice and freedom. Waiting with anticipation and expectation works this way. We hope and trust that God will enter into the space we have created, and we wait for it.

We wait expectantly.

But there's more to waiting than just expectation. There are some things we can *do* as we wait.

Wait Actively

Waiting involves much more than just sitting around and doing nothing. Waiting on God is a matter of keeping focused and staying *active* in your faith while trusting in almighty God.

Waiting actively creates God room in and from your waiting. It truly allows you to navigate the murky waters of divine distance.

Back in Esther 5:1, when Esther made her first request for the king and Haman to attend her banquet, she extended the invitation on the heels of a detail that's easily missed: it happened on the third day of fasting during which time Esther and all the Jews in Susa intentionally and intently sought God (see 4:15–17). Esther was *active* in her waiting.

This is an important aspect of waiting for us today. There are so many ways we can stay productive and active while waiting that are more than just busy work. In addition to prayer and fasting, we can actively wait by reading the Bible, serving others, worshiping God, obeying his timeless commandments, and sharing the good news of Jesus with others. This kind of active waiting isn't the cessation of activity but the *increase* of certain kinds of activity that add purpose and meaning to our waiting. God has given us something to *do* while we wait expectantly on him.

Don't misunderstand—this kind of waiting is not a form of works. We're not trying to woo and persuade a reluctant and stubborn God. Rather, our waiting is rooted in faith that claims God's promise: "I love those who love me, and those who diligently seek me will find me" (Prov. 8:17). When we understand waiting on God in this way, it changes everything, taking us from a pessimistic, hopeless mindset to one that is optimistic, faith-building, and purposeful.

Think about your relationship with God and consider that maybe God has a plan for you as you enter into a time of waiting on him. Perhaps God wants you to diligently seek him through fasting and prayer like Esther did, or he may want you to read his Word, meet with other believers, or use the resources he's given you to serve others. When you do, you may just see your waiting time become productive time in which you grow to know God better and strengthen your inner reserves. In actively waiting, you will draw close to the One from whom you feel distant.

If there are areas in your life where you're waiting on God—struggles in your marriage, frustrations with your job, disappointments with your kids, setbacks with a persistent sin, past hurts that haven't healed, concerns with extended family, poor health, or even a long-unanswered prayer—then I encourage you to wait *actively*. Do the activities that are the hallmarks of waiting on God *with purpose*. The beauty of waiting actively is that the by-product of doing so is the development of lots of God room in your life—space where God can enter in, inhabit, and do the things that are up to him alone. His activity is worth the wait.

And as if all this weren't enough, there's a final tool God's people have in their arsenal when it comes to waiting on God.

Wait Joyfully

The idea of waiting joyfully may feel like an oxymoron, like I'm encouraging you to struggle easily or scream quietly. This isn't the case at all. Two big lies from our culture that many of us have bought into say that happiness is circumstantial and joy is situational. The Bible affirms that both happiness and joy are choices that we make independent of our circumstances and situations. Our happiness is an outgrowth of our joy, and our joy is tied directly to our faith-filled relationship with God through Jesus.

Though Esther doesn't mention joy specifically in her waiting, there will come a time very soon where the joy that flows from waiting will show itself. The Old Testament prophets, whose messages Esther would have known, clearly communicated this idea of waiting joyfully. The prophet Isaiah had a tough life: godly kings let him down, he saw his nation taken into captivity, and he had to deal with obstinate people who repeatedly frustrated him. Yet he wrote, "And it will be said in that day, 'Behold, this is our God for whom we have waited that He might save us. This is the LORD for whom we have waited; Let us rejoice and be glad in His salvation'" (Isa. 25:9 NASB).

> You can wait with eager anticipation for the yet unseen movement of God in your life and well up with joy as a result, or you can allow the difficulty of your circumstances to overwhelm you. You can choose joy.

Isaiah explained his rejoicing and gladness in waiting for a deliverance that at this point was only the subject of his dreams. He saw it on the far horizon coming someday. This experience required an unknown time of waiting, yet it nonetheless filled his heart with gladness and joy despite its apparent distance. I believe Esther and Mordecai experienced the same. It's how waiting works. As we stand before God and wait expectantly and actively upon him, joy is bound to well up in our souls.

So how do you wait on God? Are you joy*less* or joy*ful*? Don't kid yourself—you have a choice. There are no victims when it comes to choosing how to wait on God. You can wait with eager anticipation for the yet unseen movement of God in your life and well up with joy as a result, or you can allow the difficulty of your circumstances to overwhelm you. You can choose joy.

Waiting expectantly, waiting actively, and waiting joyfully will change the way you view God and transform your experience of waiting on him. Most importantly, doing so will create God room in your life where the impossible becomes possible because space has been reserved for the God who "calls into existence the things that do not exist" (Rom. 4:17).

WAY 6

Faithfulness That Delivers

Love and loyalty work hand-in-hand.

—Jeremy Gove

met Tom fifteen years ago when I was flying to a pastors event and he was flying for business. We struck up a conversation, realized we both shared a common faith, and kept on talking. When he asked me what I did and found out I was a pastor, he couldn't stop talking about his church. This man loved his local church. He had been a member of this church for decades and had served on the board multiple times.

At one point during our conversation, Tom mentioned that he had once served as the youth pastor on the staff of his church. By the time I met him, he was a successful business owner and seemed to be far from church-staff dynamics. I asked him what had happened that caused him to leave his pastoral position and start his own business. He said, "I had a disagreement with a couple of staff and board members on how best to run the youth ministry. We couldn't find common ground, so I thought it best to resign rather than have it get worse. They were close to firing me anyway, so I made the first move."

I said, "Wow. That must have been incredibly painful and disappointing. You were young. You and your wife were just starting a family. This was your church. How in the world did you ever stay at this church after something like that? There are literally hundreds of churches in your city you could have gone to. Why stay?"

"It was painful, to be sure," he said. "More painful than most would realize. And it took some years to fully recover from some of the hurt and anger. But my wife and I were clear from the start: this is our church. We love our church. It's like a family. And families have disagreements, but you hang in there and work through them. So, we did."

That's when I realized I was in the presence of a man who knew the meaning of the word *faithful*. We've stayed in touch over the years, and Tom has proven this in multiple ways to me, not only with his church but also with his family, his friends, his business partnerships, and his community.

There's something about *faithfulness* that touches all who see and experience it. Whether it's a married couple remaining faithful to each other through many decades, or a close friend who is faithful through thick and thin, we are all touched when examples of true faithfulness play out before us. We all love to see it. We all love to experience it. It rings true to the deepest parts of our souls.

The seventh and eighth chapters of Esther's story reveal another key step in the trek toward navigating the rugged terrain of God's episodic distance: our faithfulness to God.

We'll look at the one-to-one correlation between our faithful actions and God's response of drawing close. Esther and her people were about to realize the potency of faithfulness to God and how it would deliver his followers to see the light of day again.

A Picture of Faithfulness

After all that has transpired to this point in Esther's story, she finds herself in a truly wonderful position. Esther had carried out the well-laid plan that God gave her. And God had orchestrated events that were far beyond her capability to manipulate. Here, in the twelve to twenty-four intervening hours between the first and second banquets, the king was totally happy with Mordecai and curiously endeared to Esther. As a result, his pump was primed to do whatever needed to be done for his wife and his loyal friend Mordecai.

It's at the second dinner party that Esther plans to drop the bomb about Haman's plot to kill the Jews and ask the king to intervene. It's here that we arrive at the climax of the story. The outcome of this banquet will determine the fate of the Jewish people. Many things hang in the balance. The only thing that could possibly thwart Esther's plan at this point was if she or Mordecai were to somehow shrink back, chicken out, lose their nerve, and fail to follow through with the final steps in the plan. The only way to sabotage what God had to this point blessed would be for Esther or Mordecai to lose faith and fail to carry out the final touches of their well-laid plan.

The God room that Esther created with her staggered, stalling plan of two banquets over multiple days allowed God to put some key things on the table for the king to process. Things like Mordecai's loyalty, Haman's hatred of Mordecai and the Jews, and Esther's Jewish heritage. These factors made it so that the redemption of the Jews would be full and complete—deliverance from annihilation, the elimination of Haman, the endearment of the king to Esther, and increased loyalty to Mordecai. But there was an equally huge risk that it could all backfire. There was a lot more in play now than before the God room was created. As we all know, the higher the potential benefit, the higher the risk. This was true for Esther and the Jews—the God room had seen to it. All that remained now was either faithfulness or unfaithfulness. Success or failure hinged upon whether Esther's and Mordecai's next steps were faithful or faithless.

Esther chooses faithfulness:

> Now the king and Haman came to drink wine with Esther the queen. And the king said to Esther on the second day also as they drank their wine at the banquet, "What is your petition, Queen Esther? It shall be granted you. And what is your request? Even to half of the kingdom it shall be done." Then Queen Esther replied, "If I have found favor in your sight, O king, and if it pleases the king, let my life be given me as my petition, and my people as my request; for we have been sold, I and my people, to be destroyed, to be killed and to be annihilated. Now if we had only been sold as slaves, men and women, I would have remained silent, for the trouble would not be commensurate with the annoyance to the king." (Esther 7:1–4 NASB)

At the conclusion of the second meal, after the king and Haman have been served their wine, Esther finally makes her request. She reveals to Ahasuerus that her life and the lives of her people are in peril, though she does not yet disclose to the king that she is Jewish or her connection to Mordecai. This prompts the king to ask who would dare threaten to destroy his wife and her people. In a truly risky moment, Esther is faithful to complete the task required. She tells the king that the conspirator is none other than the king's second-in-command: "A foe and enemy! This wicked Haman!" (Esther 7:6).

Haman, at this point, engages in a panicked last-ditch effort to save himself, which the king interprets as a desperate attempt to assault the queen. Because he has betrayed the king by going after the queen's people, Haman is hanged from the gallows he had constructed for the public disgrace of his avowed enemy, Mordecai:

> Then Harbonah, one of the eunuchs who were before the king said, "Behold indeed, the gallows standing at Haman's house fifty cubits high, which Haman made for Mordecai who spoke good on behalf of the king!" And the king said, "Hang him on it." So, they hanged Haman on the gallows which he had prepared for Mordecai, and the king's anger subsided. (Esther 7:9–10 NASB)

The irony is rich. It's at this point in the story that engrossed readers might let out a collective sigh of relief. However, Esther and Mordecai's work isn't over yet. While Haman's execution thwarts one threat, the king had already issued an official edict permitting Haman to go forward with his evil scheme of mobilizing all Persia against the Jews (3:11). Asking Ahasuerus to revoke his edict would be unprecedented to say the least. The next step requires Esther to continue in faithfulness by revealing her connection to Mordecai and asking the king to intervene to save the Jews.

Remember, in that ancient culture the king's word was law, and once given, it couldn't be revoked. Not even the king could revoke his own edict. The only thing that could turn the tide was a *new* edict. Esther and Mordecai need the king to approve (and support with his full authority) a new edict allowing the Jewish people to defend themselves. To get to this point requires faithfulness! Esther and Mordecai must stay the course with the plan that God had paved the way to accomplish. They must persist in faithfulness, trusting God *with* the process and *in* the process.

> Faithfulness means remaining steadfast and loyal, firmly adhering to a promise you've made, a belief you've held dear, or words you've said.

From God's perspective, *faithfulness* is "being true to one's words, beliefs and promises."[1] Faithfulness means remaining steadfast and loyal, firmly adhering to a promise you've made, a belief you've held dear, or words you've said. Faithfulness involves consistency and staying power. Esther and Mordecai offer us a living picture of faithfulness through their active participation in God's plan. They created God room, and God advanced his rescue. Then, they faithfully followed through, and God faithfully moved.

Faithfulness under Attack

Faithfulness to God and his people is of high value in God's economy. As we will see in more detail shortly, it is a critical way of navigating times when God feels distant. This is important, because you and I live in a world and culture where faithfulness has not only come under attack but has lost its value in many places.

A number of years ago, an advertising executive started a new greeting card line called "The Secret Lover Collection." Available online and in greeting card aisles alongside more traditional cards, the brand uniquely appealed to people involved in adulterous affairs. One Atlanta-based divorce and family attorney said of the new cards, "It seems to me really crude to use a greeting card to celebrate what, in the 16th century, was an offense by which you would be publicly hanged in the town square."[2] Fortunately, the idea proved unsuccessful, but apparently not for lack of people taking part in extramarital relationships.

More recently, internet hackers breached a website designed to facilitate adulterous affairs and publicly posted the personal data of its thirty-two million users. The site had touted its services by bragging, "Thousands of cheating wives and cheating husbands sign up every day looking for an affair. . . . With our affair guarantee package we guarantee you will find the perfect affair partner."[3] The aftermath of the shame-filled scandal included outing those who had signed up at the website and resulted in divorces and even suicides. While you might think that such a provocative disgrace would have meant certain doom for the web service, today it has fully rebounded and even flourished, bragging about welcoming more than 750,000 new subscribers every month since the scandal broke. The site, with its tagline "Life is short. Have an affair," now counts more than sixty million users worldwide.[4]

In our increasingly secular, progressively decadent contemporary culture, marital faithfulness truly has hit on hard times.

It's not just marriage. People aren't shocked anymore when a business refuses to honor its word. We aren't bewildered by the scandal of wealthy parents who unjustly scheme to place their privileged children in elite universities and usurp other young scholars who worked hard to earn a spot. We barely blink at news of families who neglect to care for aging parents or millions of people cheating on their tax forms or elected officials caught illicitly dumping stocks to protect their own wealth or CEOs fraudulently misrepresenting their publicly traded company. Don't get me wrong, news like this still makes most people sad, but rarely is it shocking. We almost expect it in our modern world.

Think about it for a moment. Are you truly surprised any more when you hear the latest news of someone's unfaithfulness or when a new scandal tops the headlines? When was the last time you were rocked by hearing of someone's disloyalty?

It is still possible to be shaken or even wounded by someone's lack of faithfulness, but it's more difficult to shock us today because the value of faithfulness has diminished significantly within our culture. In fact, the culture's response to faithfulness has been flipped on its head. In the past, one might respond to a lack of faithfulness with forgiveness and compassion. But these reactions have been replaced by condoning and even celebrating disloyalty. Faithfulness is no longer valued and celebrated. We live in a world where it's increasingly under attack.

God Values Faithfulness

Despite this trend, know this about God: in God's economy, faithfulness—both to him and to his people—remains highly valued. He prizes faithfulness. Unlike our culture, he won't send you a greeting card celebrating your unfaithfulness or provide you a service that makes it even easier to be unfaithful. In fact, God does the opposite. He faithfully convicts and corrects unfaithfulness, and at the same time he consistently and positively responds to our faithful actions with something that makes all the difference: his movement in our lives. It's true. It is through faithfulness that we experience God.

> God rewards our faithfulness. He rewards it by doing unmistakable things deep within our souls and in our very circumstances.

The Bible is filled with promises that God rewards the faithfulness of his people. It might not happen right away—that is in our timing. It might not even be in the precise way we anticipated. But make no mistake: God, who is faithful, responds to our faithfulness to him. He moves in obvious ways when we stay the course of trusting in and following him. Faithfulness is a primary way we navigate divine distance. God rewards our faithfulness. He rewards it by doing unmistakable things deep within our souls and in our very circumstances. Both inwardly and outwardly there are tangible, spiritual *byproducts* of our faithfulness to the Lord.

The more closely we look at the story of Esther, the more we see how this is true. The details reveal how the God who is faithfully at work behind the scenes orchestrates things in response to Esther's and Mordecai's faithfulness to stay the course with their God-given plan. As this happens, they experience God in unique and meaningful ways. Let's look at a few of these ways God responded to their faithfulness.

Justice

God provides justice through faithfulness. When Esther exposes Haman as the conspirator, God sees to it that he is hanged on the same gallows he had prepared for Mordecai. Additionally, when Esther pleads for the king to do something about Haman's plot to exterminate the Jews—a plan already underway, complete with the king's seal and signature behind it—God again provides justice. A new edict supersedes Haman's genocidal effort. Ahasuerus tells Mordecai, "Now you write to the Jews as you see fit, in the king's name, and seal it with the king's signet ring; for a decree which is written in the name of the king and sealed with the king's signet ring may not be revoked" (Esther 8:8 NASB).

God provided justice for Esther and Mordecai in response to their faithfulness to stay the course even when it was difficult to do so.

Honor

In addition to dishonoring Haman, who had acted so audaciously in his response to the perceived slight by Mordecai, God also brings honor to Mordecai: "And the king took off his signet ring which he had taken away from Haman and gave it to Mordecai. And Esther set Mordecai over the house of Haman" (Esther 8:2 NASB). Ahasuerus bestows Mordecai with a position of authority and power, making him the new second-in-command over all of Persia. Because of their faithfulness, not only does God place Mordecai and Esther in positions of honor but he also brings honor to all the Jews in the land: "For the Jews there was . . . honor" (8:16 NASB).

The contrast between honor and shame in Middle Eastern culture is well known. Shame from one's enemies is profoundly dealt with when honor is restored. It's a clear sign of God's blessing as it brings equilibrium back into people's lives. Faithfulness brings honor, demonstrating in a profound way the promise of God that "those who honor me I will honor" (1 Sam. 2:30).

Protection

In addition to justice and honor, God provides protection for the Jews. "The king allowed the Jews who were in every city to gather and defend their lives, to destroy, to kill, and to annihilate any armed force of any people or province that might attack them" (Esther 8:11). The king allows the Jews to defend themselves, and he even commands his own army to assist them. God sees to it that the Jews are given the resources they need to defend themselves. He gives his strength and protection in response to their faithfulness.

Joy and Gladness

Under Haman's initial edict, the Jews throughout Persia had responded with confusion, despair, mourning, and sorrow (Esther 3:15; 4:1, 3). The edict now prepared by Mordecai brings an entirely different response:

> Then Mordecai went out from the presence of the king in royal robes of blue and white, with a large crown of gold and a garment of fine linen and purple; and the city of Susa shouted and rejoiced. For the Jews there was light and gladness and joy and honor. In each and every province and in each and every city, wherever the king's commandment and his decree arrived, there was gladness and joy for the Jews, a feast and a holiday. (Esther 8:15–17 NASB)

In the whole city of Susa, in all the provinces in every city where the edict was read, there was joy and gladness. This is reminiscent of the psalmist who wrote, "Weeping may tarry for the night, but joy comes with the morning" (Ps. 30:5). The point is clear: faithfulness to God and his people eventually brings joy to the human heart, as well as peace and contentment.

Evangelism

Through Esther's and Mordecai's faithfulness, God also causes evangelism to happen: "And many among the peoples of the land became Jews, for the dread of the Jews had fallen on them" (Esther 8:17 NASB). Though our modern culture resists fear as a motivator, it was an influential one for the people of Persia. They saw the God of the Jews move, delivering his people from evil and elevating them to a place of honor. Surely, this was a persuasive and compelling experience for the polytheistic people of that time, who were familiar with and fatigued by worshiping empty and distant gods.

Such cross-cultural evangelism didn't happen often in Old Testament times. In the New Testament, evangelism is a much more prevalent theme because of the person and mission of Jesus and his church. In ancient Israel, though, it was uncommon because God was revealing himself in, to, and through the people of Israel in a prototypical way. Here, though, as a result of Esther's and Mordecai's faithfulness, widespread evangelism occurs among the Persians.

Add it all up: God provides justice, honor, protection, joy and gladness, and evangelism—all as a result of Esther's and Mordecai's faithfulness in carrying through with what was good and right. They intervened before God on behalf of their people. Some five hundred years later, the apostle Paul would write in his letter to the Galatian church, "Let us not lose heart in doing good, for in due time we will reap if we do not grow weary" (Gal. 6:9 NASB).

It Still Works This Way Today

I've lost count of the number of times that I've seen this divine reality demonstrated in my own life as well as in the lives of those around me over the past forty years. I've had a front-row seat in seeing real and tangible results come as the divine by-products of being faithful to what God has asked. We can experience the same in our own lives:

- When we stay faithful in reading the Word of God and in talking with God in prayer, we can experience inward peace and spiritual growth.
- When we stay faithful to consistently confess our sins and maintain our closeness with God, we can experience forgiveness and the feeling of being clean before him.
- When we are faithful to maintain and develop our relationships with other Christians—what we call fellowship—even when it's hard to do so, we can experience deeper relationships as well as true and invaluable Christian friendship.
- When we stay faithful in trusting God amidst our temptations and commit to abandoning ourselves to him, we can experience his power and strength to combat our temptations and have victory over them.
- When we stay faithful to our marriage vows to our spouse—not just to fidelity in general but to

intentionally loving, honoring, and cherishing the other person—we can experience growth and intimacy with our beloved, and our love for our spouse will grow.

• When we faithfully and joyfully give back to God out of the resources with which he has blessed us—our tithes and offerings of our time, skills, abilities, finances, and even our testimonies—we can experience God's provision for us and our families over and over.

Faithfulness to God and his call truly brings some unanticipated blessings. Everything from the justice, honor, protection, joy, and external witness that Esther and her people experienced to even much more as we stay the course in following the Lord even when he feels far away. Faithfulness truly delivers.

The only caveat I must mention at this point is that faithfulness is not a quick fix that has a payoff like some sort of slot machine. God is the one who determines what kind of response he gives to your faithfulness, not you or me or anyone else. It also will come in his timing, not yours. When you have persevered in faithfulness and haven't yet seen the outcome you anticipated, the wrong thing to do is give up or abandon the effort. Instead, heed the encouragement the apostle Paul gave to the church in Corinth when he wrote, "Therefore, my beloved brethren, be steadfast, immovable, always abounding in the work of the Lord, knowing that your toil is not in vain in the Lord" (1 Cor. 15:58 NASB).

> God honors your faithfulness. His power and activity are unleashed when you're full of faith that leads you to stay the course.

God honors your faithfulness. His power and activity are unleashed when you're full of faith that leads you to stay the course. Faithfulness creates God room—and it's in this space that God will move and act in unmistakable ways.

So, where and how is God calling you to be faithful at this point in your life? What pathway has the Lord laid before you? Where does he want you to stay the course like Esther and Mordecai? It might involve your troubled marriage. It might involve your rebellious teen. It might involve some social justice issue you have a passion for. It might involve the working through of troubling emotions like anger or anxiety. There are so many potential roadblocks a fallen world puts in our way.

Faithfulness can plow through them all. It's how we navigate divine distance.

WAY 7

Handling Power

Nearly all men can stand adversity, but if you want to test a man's character, give him power.

—Abraham Lincoln

Imagine yourself in the front cart of a roller coaster slowly clack-clack-clacking its way up the initial climb. Your heart thumps faster as you move higher. Your eyes water a bit as the wind blowing at this height is more robust than what you're used to. You look down to the ground, and people look like animated action figures moving silently around. Even though you know what's about to happen, the anticipation rises with the trek upward, and you feel a bit unsettled, knowing that you're completely at the mercy of this device that was created to fling you up, down, and around in loops and twists as though your life were on the edge of peril.

Then it happens—you experience that slight pause as the brake is released and the combined weight of the carts and passengers, the height of the track you've just ascended, and the force of gravity pulling you earthward are all at their peak. This is what physicists call *potential energy*—the energy an object has because of its location relative to other objects, its position, and the relationship of its parts. We know this experience by a simpler name: *power*. Depending on your perspective, power of this variety is either thrilling or terrifying.

Most experts agree that power is essentially about *control* and *influence*. Power is the controlled use of energy. It involves using whatever resources you have at your disposal—whether they be tangible resources (like money, position, and material things) or intangible resources (like your personality, natural talents, and spiritual strengths)—to effect movement and change around you. We're all familiar with this understanding and use of power. We experience power and exercise it regularly in our lives:

- A job with authority offers the power of work responsibilities, decisions, and compensation.
- A steadily invested retirement plan offers the power to decide how and where to spend the golden years of life.
- A new car with a big engine offers power to get to your destination faster (and with more fun).
- A computer with a big hard drive and fast processer offers computation power, design power, and even the power of a competitive advantage when gaming.
- Good grades in school or when testing offer the power of an educational advantage: scholarships, acceptance into better schools, and advanced placement.

The list of the experiences we have with power is endless. We've been taught to desire and pursue power from a young age. Toddlers protect their toys. Kids in elementary school carve out space on the playground. Students in high school and college pursue power through sports and academic excellence. By the time we're young adults, we're primed and ready for a world filled with the pursuit of power. And to be sure, the world we live in is all about power in the forms of possession, advancement, acquisition, position, and prestige. If you can name other expressions of power, you can be guaranteed that people want it (or want more of it). Power is just that prominent and important in the world we live in.

The Bible and Power

It's worth noting that the Bible dedicates a lot of space to the matter of power. In fact, much of what the Bible has to say about power is both encouraging and positive. The book of Genesis discloses that the earth was created with and by the power of God's spoken word. He simply said, "Let there be . . ." and it was so (Gen. 1:3, 6, 14). That's power!

In the Old Testament, the prophets, priests, chroniclers, and kings (people who at the time were powerful relative to the rest of the people) extolled God's unmatched power.[1] The New Testament writers make it known that this power is available to believers through the indwelling presence of the Holy Spirit. Look at some of the promises God makes to his people regarding power:

- We receive God's power—the same power that was given fully to Jesus—to share his good news with others.[2]

- By daily living in the power of the Holy Spirit, we can bear much spiritual fruit.[3]
- Even when we are at our weakest and have depleted our human reserves, we can be strong in the Spirit's perfecting power; we can do all things through Christ who strengthens us.[4]
- His power makes it possible for us to live godly, joy-filled, faith-increasing lives that are pleasing to him; with his divine power, we are able to overcome fear, give comfort to others, and dwell in peace.[5]

That's a lot of power. In fact, the word *power* in all its Hebrew and Greek forms occurs nearly 300 times in the Bible. The primary Greek word, *dunamis*, occurs 123 times in the New Testament. It was such a common word back then that many English words like dynamo, dynamic, dynasty, and dynamite are all derived from it. Power is not only something our world is enamored with—it is also a reality that's intrinsic to God and shared by him with us. Power was given to humanity as a good gift, but our fallen world has certainly made a mess of it.

The challenge before us as we explore what it means to navigate times when God feels far away is how to make sense of power. How do we handle the power we have? What is the Christian's role in wielding power? What is our relationship to power? How do we use power the right way? And how does any of this relate to divine distance?

Fortunately, God answers these questions so that we can use the power entrusted to us appropriately as we navigate divine distance.

A Reversal of Power

It's easy to overlook one aspect of the setting for Esther's story. Her experience took place in the context of a significant *power imbalance*. King Ahasuerus had a significant amount of power, and the exiled Jews who were living in Persia under his reign had much less. This was his land, and they were living in it as exiles, far from their homeland. To add insult to injury, generations of Jews had also been prohibited from returning to their homes where they would have had more power. The king craved power, and he abused people with it.

The Jews were subject to his abuses of power, and as a result, they were primarily interested in survival. Matters declined rapidly when the king approved Haman's genocidal request. Suddenly, because of this power imbalance and a gross abuse of that power (arising incredibly from Haman's perceived slight by Mordecai), more than a million Jews were on the brink of extinction.

Power has tremendous potential for abuse and hurt. Most of us know this, and many of us have experienced it.

Providentially, Esther bravely stepped forward and saved her people. Because of her wise, God-led plan and influence, the king approved a new edict that not only superseded Haman's decree but also *empowered* the Jews to defend themselves. Even more impressively, the king promoted Mordecai to be Haman's replacement as second-in-command, and this afforded Esther's cousin even more resources to help the Jews defend themselves against anyone who attacked them.

It's important to see the profound way God provided for the Jewish people though Haman's original edict was still in place. In that day and culture, the king never reversed, overrode, or canceled an edict. So, at the time of the new edict, Persians all across the kingdom were preparing to participate in the government-sanctioned slaughter of the Jews. Though the new edict allowed the Jews (with the aid of the king's armies) to defend themselves, there was still a battle to be fought. There was a power struggle at hand.

The next chapter of Esther's saga opens within this power-shifting setting:

> Now in the twelfth month (that is, the month Adar), on the thirteenth day when the king's command and edict were about to be executed, on the day when the enemies of the Jews hoped to *gain the mastery over them*, it was turned to the contrary so that the Jews themselves *gained the mastery over* those who hated them. (Esther 9:1 NASB)

The four-word phrase "gain the mastery over" is translated from a single Hebrew word *shalat*, which means "to rule over; to have dominion; to have power."[6] It is a word that conveys the idea of *control*. At its essence, the word pictures someone who has enough resources—whether physical, financial, emotional, social, or relational—to get the upper hand on another, that is, to have influence and control over them.

The translation here is correct: mastery over others has been gained. The proverbial shoe is now on the other foot. Power has been transferred from one group to another. When Haman was in his position of authority, he and the Persians had all the power over the Jews. They were in a prime position to gain the mastery over the Jews because of the tremendous power inequity. Now, however, the tables have turned. God has intervened and now the Jews have power. At least, they have more power than they had. As a result, the Jews gain the mastery over the Persians who sought to kill them. Without a doubt, this part of the story is about power and control over people and things.

Moreover, the power reversal is tied to Esther and her people navigating divine distance. This transfer of power is part and parcel of God's plan to help his people experience closeness once again. In his providence, God saw fit to imbue the Jews with *power* so they could then have victory over their enemies. This provision of power would then lead them to the closeness with him that their hearts had been longing for. Instead of merely knowing and trusting God in his transcendence, they would experience him in his immanence. We'll see this reality in the celebration that comes on the heels of their victory—a celebration that still occurs today in Jewish communities.

At this point in the story, however, the victory and celebration are only potential. The Jewish people's experience of God's closeness hinges on how they will use the power God gave them. Handling power was key to closing the gap they felt with God. The right use of power would allow them to navigate rightly that time when God felt far away. The same will be true for us.

You've Got the Power

Before we look at how we need to handle power in our lives in order to best navigate spiritually dry seasons, we must first discover a key truth in Esther's and Mordecai's experience: *God gives each of us a relative amount of power that is available for us.* Even when our chips are down, we still have power. Remember our definition of power. Each and every one of us has a certain amount of *control* given the *resources* we have available in our daily lives. Whenever we use our resources (the tangible ones like money and position as well as the intangible ones like our thoughts, emotions, and words) to exert influence positively or negatively on the people and things around us, we are using our power.

Let me show you what I mean. In the story of Esther, at each successive stage, it's important to recognize that each player has some measure of influence and control. They *all* have some power. Mordecai has some power. Esther has some power. The Jews have some power. The Persians also have some power. The king definitely has some power. Virtually everyone has *some* power.

> God gives each of us a relative amount of power that is available for us.

Even when the tide of power seems overwhelmingly against them and the chips are down, Esther and her people have power. They have power to plan, pray, fast, mobilize, communicate together, do right things, and make good decisions—all the things we've been looking at that helped them navigate divine distance. Their power resulted from the use of the resources God had blessed them with.

They had *some* power. After the tide turns in Esther 9, they have *more* power than they had before, but this is only because of a shift in power, not an absence of power at any point.

It's important to glean from this story that we all have power. Because we are made in the image of God and are living and breathing today, each of us has power. I call this *creation power*. We can exert our will, and we have the ability to act. We can influence others and exercise a degree of control. Even when circumstances are against us (like they were with the Jews in the early chapters of our story), we still have the God-given ability to act, think, feel, relate, and pray. Esther and Mordecai did, and it paid off.

If you're a follower of Jesus, you have an even further (and more potent) form of power, what I call *Spirit power*. The Bible makes it clear that the Holy Spirit lives in those who believe in and follow Jesus, and this indwelling Spirit becomes a source of power. "You will receive power when the Holy Spirit has come upon you" (Acts 1:8). The strength to resist sin, the ability to profoundly forgive others, the wisdom for understanding the things of God, discernment for traversing this crazy world, the faith to endure hardship—these are all available to you through the Holy Spirit as you believe in and follow Jesus.

The point is, though you may not have as much power as you'd like in certain areas of your life, don't think for a moment that you have no power. Even if you have been hurt and victimized by others with more power, you still have power. At the very least, you have personal, spiritual power as you lean on the God who's actively at work behind the scenes of your life.

What's important to understand then is that God's chief concern is *not* that you have power (because he knows that we all have some power); instead, his concern is what you do with the power he has given you. I learned this truth when I was a young adult in my midtwenties. Unlike some overly confident, full-of-spit-and-wind young people, I was the opposite. I was filled with anxiety and fear—insecure much of the time as a young pastor. I was intimidated by most of the people around me. I felt that I was a mess while they had their act together. I was terrified of failure and even more terrified of success, virtually paralyzed with fear. I felt powerless. It revealed itself in just about every area of my life. From my public speaking to my pastoral leadership to my interpersonal relationships, I felt that I had little control and no resources for change.

Most psychologists would tell you that this is the recipe for feeling like a victim, and I certainly felt and acted like one. I ping-ponged between defensive anger at those around me and loathsome self-hatred. As one of my close friends conveyed to me, I came across as "an egomaniac with an inferiority complex." One minute I was artificially lifting myself up to get the upper hand on those around me; the next minute, I was groveling in low self-esteem. It was only through God's amazing grace and truth poured out through his Word, a few wise and faithful friends, my wife, my pastoral mentors, and a seasoned counselor that I began to realize that even with my years of hurt and baggage I had more personal and spiritual power than I realized. I had more *resources* at my disposal to exert *control* over my circumstances than I understood. Creation power combined with Spirit power is a potent force.

It was at this point that I began to change. It didn't occur overnight, but I moved out of a victim mindset and into a right understanding of how God had equipped me to live. I grew ready to harness the personal and spiritual power God had given to me. And God hasn't just given that power to me but to all who will recognize the natural and spiritual resources he provides. In short, I was ready to learn how to *handle* the power that was in my soul and life, and handling power would prove to be formidable in helping me learn how to effectively deal with seasons when God seemed more behind the scenes than front and center. Recognizing power is one thing; learning to handle it rightly is another. Both are crucial to drawing close to the Lord and experiencing his presence and activity in our lives.

How to Handle Power

One of the first things I learned as a young man in recovery mode was that the more power one has, the more difficult it is to handle. Each of us has power, and once we recognize this, the battle is then not to let that power become unwieldy. God is greatly concerned that we each handle the power entrusted to us well. It will make or break our experience of him.

In the late 1800s, a Cambridge University professor named John Dalberg-Acton became known for his vast knowledge of political history and practice. He was widely respected for his wisdom and insight and was honored as a baron by Queen Victoria. In his writings, he observed that whenever people acquired too much power, bad things tended to happen. Whether it was Attila the Hun, Napoleon, Louis XVI, Richard I, or even the pope (Acton himself was a faithful Catholic), they all proved the tendency of power's corrupting nature. In writing to Mandell Creighton, the archbishop of the Church of England, on the topic of how historians should evaluate the morality of past leaders, he argued that the practice of judging leaders through moral relativism was inadequate. Instead, leaders should be held to a universal moral standard. In making his case, Acton famously wrote, "The danger is not that a particular class is unfit to govern. Every class is unfit to govern. . . . Power tends to corrupt, and absolute power corrupts absolutely."[7]

History has proven him right. There's something about the corrupting nature of power that should cause all of us to be cautious. Having the resources necessary to control circumstances and other people is not bad in and of itself, as it's patterned after God and originally given by him to all people for good purposes. But if we're not careful, power can quickly turn on us and deeply hurt those around us.

Esther's story affirms this principle. When the weight of power shifted dramatically from being against Esther, Mordecai, and the Jews to then being *for* or *with* them, they didn't reject its advantage: "The Jews struck down all their enemies with the sword, killing and destroying them, and they did what they pleased to those who hated them. In the citadel of Susa, the Jews killed and destroyed five hundred men" (Esther 9:5–6 NASB).

Though it sounds harsh—and was—their use of power went even further. The Bible details how they ensured that Haman's ten sons were killed, and as the king granted them to do so, how the Jews killed many more people the next day. Reading about this carnage could make it easy for us to be critical of the Jewish people's use of power. To be fair, though, you have to remember that immediately prior to this, the entire region had been preparing to slaughter the more than one million Jews in Persia by way of government-backed genocide. In fact, a closer look at the details of the Jews' warfare shows that all their actions were defensive in nature: "Meanwhile, the remainder of the Jews who were in the king's provinces also assembled to *protect themselves and get relief from their enemies*" (9:16 NIV).

Most expert Bible commentators affirm that the Jews were fighting for their lives, so even when they struck first (as is reported in verses 5–6), they did so with full knowledge that these people were preparing an imminent advance on them with intent to kill.

Even so, there's no mistaking that Mordecai and the Jews, who were only recently struggling for power, now found themselves wielding an incredible amount. They had the king's new edict, the provincial leaders, and the royal army all behind them. They even had the king's permission, as verse 5 explains, to do "as they pleased to those who hated them." Ironically, this is the exact wording that was used when the king gave Haman permission to destroy all the Jews: "The king said to Haman, 'The silver is yours, and the people also, to do with them as you please'" (3:11 NASB).

We know exactly what Haman intended to do with the power that was given to him, and it ultimately led to his own destruction. Not only did that power prove tragically unmanageable for Haman, but it resulted in a complete reversal of power with his intended prey, the Jews, who now had the very same amount of power that had once been entrusted to him. And because they now had massive power, they ran the same risk that befell Haman: the more power you have, the harder it is to handle.

This is the simple truth about power. It's not easy to handle. And the more you have of it, the harder handling it is.

Think about the power you've been given in your own life. When times are stressful, you are most vulnerable to misusing the power you have. It's in those moments when things are going badly at work that you are more inclined to be short with your spouse or kids. It's in those seasons when your home life is tense that you are more likely to treat your coworkers poorly. Even when you have good intentions to use one part of your life as a temporary escape from the other, life isn't so neatly compartmentalized. The spillover stress from the one part of your life affects how you treat others in another part. Stress from one domain can cause a misuse of power in another.

Consider the power you have right now in your life. Think about the power dynamics in your various relationships:

- With your child, who might be doing great, might be rebelling, or might simply be struggling with an important part of their life.

- With your coworkers; this includes the people supervising you (fairly or unfairly) and people that you lead (who are either following well or poorly).
- With your spouse, whom you promised to love, honor, and cherish till death do you part; you're either thriving together, just maintaining, or worse yet, seeking to escape from mutual misery.
- With your community where you lead or serve; you may find it deeply rewarding or deeply frustrating.
- With your church, where you feel vibrantly plugged in or woefully disconnected.
- With your friends, people whom you may trust and value or perhaps barely know and tolerate.
- With your God, who feels either intimately near or disturbingly distant.

Recognize the power that's available to you right now. Grasp the profound responsibility you bear to manage the power that has been entrusted to you in the expressions and experiences of your different relationships. Like Mordecai and Esther who could do what they pleased with those around them, most of us have tremendous freedom and choice in how to respond to the people in our lives.

We have great power in how we choose to deal with the most important relational and spiritual experiences we face in our daily world.

Think about it: we have the power to love or hate; to hurt or heal; to protect from pain or inflict it upon others. We have the power to destroy or rekindle and rebuild. We have the power to walk with God in such a way that his Holy Spirit rises up within us and resources us for victory—what Christians of old called "vivifying the Spirit"—or to shrink back and let the circumstances around us win the day. We have great power in how we choose to deal with the most important relational and spiritual experiences we face in our daily world. Surely, the more power you have, the harder it is to handle that power wisely and well.

It All Comes Down to Tempering Your Power

In classic warfare, the broadsword was a vital piece of weaponry. Unlike the thinner, lighter rapier used for dueling, the broadsword is heavy, flat, and double-edged. It's made for inflicting major damage in battle. It's important for the broadsword to be heavy enough to maximize the force of the one who wields it, but not so heavy that it can't be handled deftly and used both offensively and defensively. Just as important: the ideal broadsword must be hard, not brittle, so that its edges stay sharp enough to penetrate an enemy's metal armor and strong enough to deflect that enemy's repeated blows without dulling. However, sometimes imperfections could develop during a sword's forging—when the blade was heated (to the point where the crystal structure of the metal changed) and then quenched, or rapidly cooled, to harden it.

To protect against this risk, blacksmiths subjected broadswords to a *tempering* process that followed the hardening process. Tempering a sword involves reheating it (after it's quenched) to a slightly less intense heat and then allowing it to cool naturally. Tempering allows the metal's complex crystals to cool into a solid with structural integrity. This increases the weapon's strength, toughness, hardness, impact resistance, and wear resistance while decreasing its brittleness, plasticity, and elasticity. A well-tempered weapon is durable, reliable, and effective. So, *cooling* a hot metal is key to its strength.

In a similar way, power that's heated unwisely can be flawed, faulty, and even fragile (even if it's also unwieldly because of its immensity). Like a good broadsword, power must be tempered. Its heat must be monitored and controlled. Esther's story shows three distinct ways that the Jewish people tempered the nearly unbridled power that had been given to them in the king's do-as-you-please edict.

First, as I noted earlier in this chapter, the Jewish people assumed a defensive posture. They "gathered to defend their lives" (Esther 9:16). They weren't haphazard. Instead, they only attacked those who were bent on destroying them.

Second, they only attacked men. The text says, "And in Susa the citadel itself the Jews killed and destroyed 500 men . . . the ten sons of Haman were hanged . . . and they killed 300 men in Susa" (9:6, 14–15). The text uses the Hebrew word for "men" rather than "people" to make this point. The Jewish people didn't touch women or children—only men. Battle-hardened, bent-on-killing-them men.

Third, and most fascinatingly, they did not take any material possessions or land from those they killed. The chapter makes the point three times over: "but they laid no hands on the plunder" (9:10, 15, 16). Though Haman's plan was to plunder them, and though the king pointedly told them they had every right to do this, and he even encouraged them to plunder (8:11), the Jews chose not to reap any material gain from their victory.

Let's review: defensive posture only; no women or children hurt; and no material gain—three key restraints for a blank check of power. And we have to ask, "Why? Why would the Jews act with such self-control and moderation?" What just about every Bible expert posits is this: it was because of obedience to and love for the God who was behind the scenes. Even though God felt distant (and in many ways was distant), the Jewish people knew that obedience to him required *tempering* their power.

Navigating divine distance depended in it.

Murdering innocent people is wrong—the sixth commandment in God's top ten prohibits it. Killing those who were not part of Haman's plot, as well as killing family members of those who plotted against them, would have been wrong. As far as plunder is concerned, some point out that 1 Samuel 15 was most likely in play. That's where Saul explicitly went against God's command and took plunder from his defeated enemies—and God wasn't happy. As a result, the Jews in Persia didn't do that. Plundering their enemies wouldn't have honored God.

In short, it was *God's grace and truth* that tempered the otherwise unwieldy power that had been given to the Jews. God's grace and truth gave them wisdom and led them to handle their power rightly—so that they were protected without needlessly harming others.

Thomas Jefferson, the third president of the United States and one of the nation's founding fathers, once said, "I hope our wisdom will grow with our power, and teach us the less we use our power the greater it will be."[8] The Jews in Persia put this idea into action, using less power than they could have. As a result of the way they rightly handled power, God honored them with great success. And as we will see in this next chapter, this also made them ready to celebrate the deliverance God provided and helped them to feel close to him once again.

What About You?

Evaluate your own use of the power God has given you. Are you thoughtlessly, or even forcefully, imposing it upon those around you, creating a swath of hurt and damage in your wake? Or, are you seeking God's truth and grace to temper the power he's given you, believing that your power will be stronger and more honorable by far than any power you might exercise apart from him?

Be guided by his love as it is expressed as grace and truth. In the use of your power, exercise it wisely and rightly. If you aren't able to make a fair judgment about how you handle your power, ask the people in your life who are affected by it. Have a frank talk with your spouse, your kids, or your colleagues. Get some feedback on how you're wielding the power allotted to you.

Remember the apostle Paul's words to his protégé, Timothy, when mentoring the young man in spiritual leadership. He wrote: "For God has not given us a spirit of timidity, but of power and love and discipline" (2 Tim. 1:7 NASB). Paul's words to Timothy affirm that power is to be tempered by grace (love) and truth (discipline).

Power without these characteristic strengtheners is nothing more than the power that's common to the rest of the world, equally as dangerous to the user as it is to the people in its path. Power tempered with grace and truth, though, honorably protects and preserves those who wisely and rightly use it. And it leads us closer to him.

WAY 8

Celebrating the Victories

I think the important thing now is to have a celebration and then with determination move into our common, shared, different future.

—Michael D. Higgins, president of Ireland (2011–20)

When the clock strikes midnight on January 1, people all around the world celebrate New Year's Day. Fireworks exploding a panorama of color in the night skies, music blaring in public venues, and masses of people hugging, kissing, and reveling together—the entire world is a collection of parties with the global population marking the successful completion of the old year and looking forward to making the year ahead the best yet.

People are no strangers to celebration. On a personal level, we celebrate births, marriages, employment anniversaries, and more. On a national level, we have established holidays around significant events (Independence Day, Patriots' Day,

147

Juneteenth), historic people (Presidents' Day, Martin Luther King Jr. Day), important remembrances (Thanksgiving Day, Memorial Day), and traditional and modern values (Mother's Day, Father's Day). We throw parties to celebrate different cultures (Mardi Gras, Kwanzaa, Cinco de Mayo, Oktoberfest), sporting events (such as Super Bowl Sunday and the Kentucky Derby, where the parties are as famous as the actual events), and particular causes both trivial (Groundhog Day, April Fools' Day) and important (Election Day). We even add celebratory flair to days that have traditionally been stressful or unpleasant to make them more appealing (Black Friday, Cyber Monday). According to the website NationalDayCalendar.com, which claims to be the place "Where the World Gathers to Celebrate Every Day," the annual calendar is filled with close to fifteen hundred overlapping days, weeks, and months that highlight national or international celebrations of one kind or another.

What most of us might not realize is that for the Western half of the world these habits and practices are rooted in patterns seen in the Old Testament—patterns that were unique in their day compared with other contemporary cultures but that became less typical in New Testament times. The history of the people of God as recorded in the Old Testament shows that whenever God did something unique or powerful in the life of an individual or the community as a whole, they would commemorate the event either by giving a special name to the place where it happened, by associating the event with a symbol for future reference, or by instituting a special feast that the people would partake in on the commemorative day. In other words, the people of God would consistently do something tangible and special to mark the occasion of what God had done—to always remember what God had done—that would also empower them to pass it on to the next generation. They would celebrate.

In the book of Genesis, Abraham obeyed God's command to sacrifice his son Isaac. But at the last moment, God intervened by providing a ram for the sacrifice instead of his son. This was a test of Abraham's faith, and Abraham passed. To memorialize what God did there, Abraham named the place Jehovah Jireh, which in Hebrew means "the Lord will provide" (Gen. 22:14). That place was a reminder for him of God's provision.

Years later, Abraham's grandson Jacob struggled with God about the call on his life to lead his people who would one day become a nation. After one night of literally wrestling with God, Jacob was a changed man. He was physically changed by his encounter, but the even bigger change was his willingness to follow God in the details of his life. Jacob named the place of this encounter Peniel, meaning "God's face" (Gen. 32:30), because Jacob saw God's face and lived. From that point, everybody who visited Peniel would remember God's special activity that happened there.

Later still, during the Exodus event when God powerfully delivered the Jewish people from slavery in Egypt, there was one particular night when the final plague took place and all the firstborn in Egypt were killed as a sign to Pharaoh to bring an end to his stubbornness and let God's people go free. Yet, the Jewish people who obediently sacrificed an unblemished lamb and spread the lamb's blood over the door and down the doorposts saw their children spared from the angel of death. In the thirty-five hundred years since then, the Jewish people have celebrated Passover, which is marked by an annual feast and an array of different symbols that powerfully communicate aspects of God's character and his amazing work of deliverance at that time in their history.

Then, one of my personal favorites: many years after the Israelites first inhabited the Holy Land, when the dreaded Philistines were waging war against Israel, God moved unmistakably in answer to the prophet Samuel's prayer for victory. In celebration of the victory he gave, Samuel found an ordinary rock and placed it smack-dab in the middle of the battlefield. He named the rock Ebenezer, which means, "stone of help," because God had clearly helped them, and he was their Rock (1 Sam. 7:12). The rock was a symbol of God's movement and activity in their midst.

Time and again, God moved in special ways in the lives of the Jews. Instead of moving on quickly and forgetting what God had done for them, they paused, instituted a simple-but-profound action associated with what God had done, and then committed to return regularly to remember his action and celebrate it. The Jewish people—then and now—have always been known as a culture that delights in symbols and celebrations. They have hundreds of traditions and actions they regularly engage in to remember and reflect upon God's great acts through the ages.

Remembering and reflecting have long been effective ways to navigate times of divine distance. Through periods of intense persecution, spiritual dryness, and difficult circumstances, the Jewish people have been able to remember and reflect on the amazing movement of God in their history, which has given them strength to endure. Remembering and reflecting helped to bridge the gap between the times of spiritual anemia they experienced and the life-giving sense of God's presence, which enabled them to persevere. Celebration works this way. It becomes a key pathway for navigating divine distance.

It's fitting therefore that the story of Esther concludes with a celebration. This teaches us an important principle: whenever God moves uniquely and powerfully in our lives, it is worth celebrating.

The Celebration of the Jews' Victory in Persia

Let's do a quick review so that we're clear on what has happened to this point. The action has ping-ponged between bad news and good news. The story began with the people of Israel in their fourth generation of exile, having been banished far from their homeland to a hostile nation to the northeast. Bad news. That's followed by some good news: the Persian king Ahasuerus chose a humble Jewish woman named Esther to be his new bride. Next, Esther's cousin Mordecai angered Haman, the king's second-in-command, by refusing to bow before him. As a result, Haman schemed to kill Mordecai and to annihilate all the Jews in Persia for good measure. However, Esther sought God, fasted before him, and advanced a godly plan, inviting the king and Haman to banquets on two consecutive nights.

At the end of the second feast, God, who was behind the scenes, orchestrated events so that the king favorably responded to Esther, Mordecai, and the Jews. The king had Haman hanged for his diabolical plot, empowered the Jews to defend themselves against the impending Persian advance, and even supplemented their forces with his own army. After two days of battle, the Jews overwhelmingly defeated their foes, Mordecai was named second-in-command, and all the Jews in Persia could once again rest without fear of impending death.

Now, instead of retreating to their homes, Mordecai and Esther declare, "It's party time!"

> Then Mordecai recorded these events, and he sent letters to all the Jews who were in all the provinces of King Ahasuerus, both near and far, obliging them to celebrate the fourteenth day of the month Adar, and the fifteenth day of the same month, annually, because on those days the Jews rid themselves of their enemies, and it was a month which was turned for them from sorrow into gladness and from mourning into a holiday; that they should make them days of feasting and rejoicing and sending portions of food to one another and gifts to the poor. (Esther 9:20–22 NASB)

In the full light of God's rescue and deliverance, Esther and Mordecai determine that it is the right time to pause, reflect, remember, and celebrate. They institute a new tradition that will forever remind future generations about God's unique and powerful victory. They give the celebration a name highlighting a unique detail of how God delivered his people from Haman's diabolical plan. Haman had cast lots to choose a day as Kill-All-the-Jews Day. The Jewish people therefore decide to call their new celebration Purim after the Babylonian custom of using homemade dice (*purim*) for decision-making: "Therefore they called these days Purim after the name of Pur" (Esther 9:26 NASB).

For twenty-five hundred years the Jewish people have celebrated the Purim holiday. Through good times and bad, through times of plenty and times of lack, each generation has observed this annual celebration. Occurring in the month of Adar on the Jewish calendar, Purim usually falls during March. As part of this celebration, Jewish people engage in five primary activities to remember what is recorded in the book of Esther:

- *Fasting.* The day before they celebrate, the Jews fast for one full day from sunup to sundown, just as Esther and the Jews fasted prior to God's deliverance. The first activity done to celebrate the work of God is a spiritual activity.

- *Remembering and reliving the story.* On the day of Purim, the Jewish people read the entire book of Esther aloud. This is known as the *megillah*, from the Hebrew word for "scroll." The story is read for all to hear. Everyone present to hear the story has in their hand a *gragger*, a loud and obnoxious noisemaker that they whirl every time the name of Haman is read. The effect is to drown or blot out his name. Haman's name is mentioned over fifty times in the story, so it becomes quite a ruckus when the story is read.

- *Feasting.* The Jews then enjoy being merry as they eat and drink together.

- *Gift exchange.* They exchange gifts with one another and even make little "Haman cakes" (*hamantaschen*) to recall the significance of God's deliverance.

- *Charitable giving.* As an overflow of their gratitude to God, the Jews also intentionally give gifts to the poor.

Take note: Purim is a high-energy celebration that is carnival-like in some Jewish communities. In fact, some authors refer to Purim as "Jewish Mardi Gras." Truly, Purim is a positive, joy-filled party marked by laughter, rejoicing, and revelry. And for the right reasons. God came through for the Jews. He protected his people.

Remember, too, that Purim is celebrated in addition to the many other holidays and traditions that fill the Jewish calendar. Virtually all of the holidays and commemorations are linked to unique and powerful movements of God in the lives of the Jewish people (almost all of which are recorded in the Old Testament).

What Gives?

So, here is my question: with this obvious and overt emphasis the Jewish people have placed upon remembering through celebration, *Why don't Christians celebrate like this more often? Why don't we follow the Old Testament patterns in our personal lives and in our churches and communities?*

To be sure, we have the symbols of the cross and the fish, and we make a big deal out of Christmas and Easter. To some degree, we understand the importance of setting aside special moments to celebrate the keystone events of our faith. Some traditions also include observances from the subdued to the festive, days and seasons like Advent, Palm Sunday, Ash Wednesday, Good Friday, Pentecost, and several others.

Even so, we pale by comparison to the pattern set in the Old Testament, where the Jewish people seem to memorialize and celebrate *wherever and whenever* God moved in unique and powerful ways. Jewish tradition is like the Ferrari of celebration compared to our little Fiat. There's nothing wrong with a Fiat (I've owned a few, and I like them); it's just that it doesn't compare to a Ferrari.

When I read in the Old Testament about all the wonderful and various symbols and celebrations God's people developed—right in the moment of God's unique and wonderful movement—I begin to long for this kind of intentionality in our day and age among the followers of Jesus. I want Christians to party more!

We have so much to be glad about and celebrate, whether in our own personal lives or in our churches and spiritual communities. We could use more celebration when God moves in our midst. Celebrating serves as a marker that we can look to time and again when our spiritual light grows dim.

Let's Amass Some Rocks

If you were to come into my office and meet with me for a conversation, you would look behind my conference table and see the wall where I keep my library, a few thousand books I've accumulated over years of learning and serving as a pastor. On the far-right side of my library, there's also a large shelf with a bunch of knickknacks on it. People are always interested when they pore over that shelf to learn what a particular item is, and they're even more interested in learning the story behind an item—why it's something I decided to save and display on the shelf.

Everything that's displayed there has meaning and value to me. In a real sense, those knickknacks are my remembrances; each one is an Ebenezer like Israel's celebratory and commemorative stone of help that reminded them of God's battlefield provision in their wartime need. The items are the proverbial rocks I have placed in the battlefield of my life, commemorating what God has done either in my life or in the life of the people

I've been honored to shepherd. They help me remember what God has done. They remind me of the movement of God. They help me recall and celebrate. When I'm feeling spiritually blue and down in the dumps, I'll walk over to this shelf, pick up an item or two, and then remember and reflect on the profound movement of God in history past.

Among the items there's a row of a half dozen antique fire-suppression sprinklers that were taken out of different buildings. Each of the sprinklers was given to me one or two at a time by a friend in Cleveland whom I had the honor of pastoring many years ago.

My friend was a firefighter. He started as part of a squad, then was promoted to chief, and then became the head of the entire department for his town. Ultimately, he became an arson investigator. One day he asked if I could grab lunch with him, so I did.

When I asked him what had brought him so far out of the way to our church, he said that it was a difficult series of events that had brought him there. For twenty years he had attended a different church nearer to where he lived. He was very involved there and had become close friends with the pastor. He eventually became the chairman of the board of that church.

At one point, there was an accusation made against his pastor by a woman who claimed to have had an affair with him. No one could imagine the accusation being true. My friend went to his pastor and asked him if it was. The pastor denied the accusation and said the woman was making up lies. Though he was asked numerous times, the pastor maintained his story that he never had inappropriate relations with this woman. Even when my friend looked him straight in the eye and asked directly, the pastor replied, "I did not. She is lying."

But after months of discussion and investigation, as the heat kept being turned up, the pastor eventually broke. In front of the congregation, he admitted, "It's true." He had been having an affair with this woman. In addition to his immoral behavior, this pastor had lied to my friend, the chairman of the board, looking him in the eye and betraying him. To add insult to injury, my friend had defended the pastor in front of the congregation during his denial. He had believed him, trusted him, and put everything on the line for him.

As you can imagine, this was devastating to the church. Not only were they mad at the pastor, some of them were also mad at the board because my friend, as chairman, had publicly defended the pastor. He had put his own reputation on the line only to find out later that the pastor had been lying. My friend told me that the entire situation became unbearable for him and his wife. Their names were tarnished among the congregation, and they felt like the best option they had for the sake of the church was to leave and go somewhere different where they could start anew.

After he told me this story, I said, "Why in the world would you want to get close to me?"

Think about it: This man had just been burned. He had been deeply hurt by a pastor who lied to him and betrayed his trust. He stuck his neck out for his friend and pastor, only to be badly wounded in doing so. If I were in his shoes and had been hurt as deeply, I don't know whether I could do what he was doing right then with me. While I don't think for a moment that I'd forsake Jesus over something like this, in all honesty I'd be hard pressed to leap back into a church and trust a pastor again if I had been wounded the way my friend was. Yet here this man was trying to get to know me better.

So I asked again, "After your experience, why are you wanting to get to know me?"

He answered, "You have to understand, Jamie, that I love Jesus. But I also love his church. Yes, I've been wounded deeply. But I'm never, ever going to give up on his church. You might let me down someday too. I hope you don't. Even if you do, I'll give it another try again, because this is not about me. This is about God and his church."

Over the years, I've accumulated more stories than I ever wanted to know from people who have been wounded by their church. It grieves me every day. There are so many stories out there about spiritual casualties that it makes me try to mind my attitude and actions. The reality is, when I heard my friend tell me about his tenacious faith in God and even in God's church, I was moved in my spirit. Only God could accomplish what he had in my friend's life.

From that first meeting, every time I would meet with my friend, he'd give me a new sprinkler or two. I don't know why, because I'm not really into them. But as he would bring them, I kept them and set them apart as an Ebenezer. When I look at them, I remember the fires that erupted in his life as a result of being deeply wounded, and I think about how God poured his Spirit over my friend like soothing, calming water to put out those flames. Every time I see the sprinklers in my office, I think of my friend, and I think about the move of God in his life, and I think to myself, "Only God!" The movement of God in his life has been powerful enough to move me, and still many years later it affects me.

I could tell you more stories of the other Ebenezers I have in my office and at home. Each one represents a memorable, significant, unique, and powerful way that God has moved in my life and in the lives of others. While the details change with each Ebenezer, the point is the same: Christians need to celebrate more! We need to tangibly mark our celebrations so that we will always remember what God has done and intentionally revisit these meaningful experiences. Remembrance gives way to celebration. Ebenezers become reasons to party.

Celebrating to Bridge the Gap

Over the years I've found that remembering and celebrating God's unique movement in our lives—and even commemorating the events with some sort of symbol or party—is a great way to navigate times of divine distance. Celebrations shore us up when the chips are down. They remind us that there was a day when God was in the forefront. They remind us that those days will come again.

Esther's story offers two guiding principles that should flavor and influence any and all celebrations God's people choose to have. They help us make sure our partying is done in such a way that allows us to navigate divine distance.

We Celebrate to Remember and Honor

We celebrate to remember what God has done in our midst and to honor him as the one who has done it. The Jewish people embodied this principle in their Purim celebration:

So, these days were to be *remembered* and *celebrated* throughout every generation, every family, every province and every city; and these days of Purim were not to fail from among the Jews, or *their memory fade* from their descendants. (Esther 9:28 NASB)

It's as though the author of this historical account is saying with editorial insight, "We do this so we will never forget what God has done in our midst—never forget where we almost ended up but for God's movement and activity in our lives. We do this so we will remember that where we are now is due to his unique and powerful grace."

> **Kingdom celebrations are designed to remember and honor what God has done in our lives.**

Just as birthdays commemorate the day we were born or anniversaries honor the day we were married, kingdom celebrations are designed to remember and honor what God has done in our lives. This is the top priority. If your celebration doesn't remember and honor what God has done in your life, it is *not* a kingdom party. Without this priority, your celebration is no different than your annual company picnic or end-of-year office party. But with this priority, you're going to get in touch with the God who has always loved you and wants you to see the light of day again.

We Celebrate Spiritually and Relationally

This second principle is both critical and distinctive, especially given our modern culture's emphasis on independence and individuality:

[Mordecai] sent letters to all the Jews . . . to establish these days of Purim at their appointed times, just as Mordecai the Jew and Queen Esther had established for them, and just as they had established for themselves and for their descendants with instructions for their times of *fasting and their lamentations.* (Esther 9:31 NASB)

Then Mordecai recorded these events, . . . because on those days the Jews rid themselves of their enemies, and it was a month which was turned for them from sorrow into gladness and from mourning into a holiday; that they should make them days of feasting and rejoicing and sending portions of food *to one another* and *gifts to the poor*. (9:22 NASB)

Spirituality and relationality are the two key values in these verses. Notice that the Jews' celebration had a spiritual foundation to it (fasting and prayers of lamentation) and it had a relational expression (they gave food and gifts to one another). The Jewish celebrations almost always had a focus upon God and what he had done in their lives as well as an activity that went along with this such as fasting, lamenting, praying, singing, or serving. Moreover, their celebrations were hardly ever done alone. They were done in community and with others in mind.

Kingdom celebrations are different from other celebrations. A class reunion may offer a chance for people to get together, remember days of old, and catch up, but they rarely have a meaningful spiritual component to them. Kingdom celebrations must have components that are both relational and spiritual. They must honor and remember what God has so uniquely and powerfully done.

Let's Party!

If God has saved you from sin and its eternal consequences, then you have reason to party. If he's brought hope and healing into your marriage, you have reason to party. If he has freed you from addiction, you have reason to party. If he's reconciled an important relationship, you have reason to party. If he has given you renewed purpose and hope on this side of heaven, you have reason to party. If he's calmed the rage within you, quieted the doubt that disturbed you, or brought peace to the troubles within you, you have reason to party. If he has caused you to be less self-obsessed and more focused on others in need, you have reason to party.

Whenever and however God has moved uniquely and powerfully in your life, you have reason to party. Jesus said that whenever a person repents (that is, turns away from a life of sin and back toward God), "there is rejoicing in the presence of the angels of God" (Luke 15:10 NIV). We can join and add to this rejoicing as we likewise celebrate the amazing movements of God on earth. And we will feel closer to God when we do.

AFTERWORD

The Ways Surpass the Formula

When we began this journey, I promised we'd spend more time on the solutions than we would outlining the problem. The problem is obvious and glaring: many of us experience seasons when God feels far away. Sometimes long seasons. Sometimes even at a chronic, rather than acute, level. We might not talk about it—especially not around Christians who come across like eighth-century mystics who constantly feel the Lord's presence—but we know deep down what's in our souls, and many times it's an experience of divine distance.

The story of Esther delivers on the promise for solutions. If any group of people in the Bible were connoisseurs of perceived distance from God, it was the Jews living in exile. Yet their journey depicts eight key ways to navigate divine distance. Eight ways that allowed them to experience the closeness of God once again.

In short, these ways work. They worked for Esther and her people, and they've worked over the last twenty-five hundred years for millions of almighty God's followers. The real benefit is that they work when the chips are down. They work when our spiritual walk is at a crawl. They work when we feel that our reserves are low, and our spiritual horsepower isn't enough for the climb ahead.

During the height of the COVID-19 pandemic in 2020, I needed to get from where I live in Arizona to Michigan. I didn't feel comfortable flying, and my brother in Michigan needed a car, so I decided to drive a car from Arizona to Michigan. It was a good little car—emphasis on *little*. It was a late-model Fiat 500. These Fiats are small, compact cars that get great gas mileage because they need only a small engine. I learned, however, that while this car was great for driving around town, it wasn't as strong in mountainous terrain. Phoenix is in a valley. The only way out is to climb from the valley floor to the top of what's called the Mogollon Rim. From there, it's smooth sailing across the Midwest to Michigan.

The challenge is that the climb to the top of the rim is fifty-five hundred feet. As you can imagine, there are some long, steep hills. When faced with one of these, I placed the car in third gear (out of five) and put the pedal to the floor, but the car kept slowing down. I was unable to keep up with even the slowest traffic. Semitrucks were passing me. The good news is that I made it—barely. While navigating up one of these hills, I found myself wishing I had invested in the Abarth version of the Fiat 500. The Abarth is the performance model, and it has a turbocharger attached to the engine that increases the horsepower significantly. It makes a slow, underpowered Fiat into a little rocket. I longed for that rocket.

Life is sometimes like a steep, uphill climb. More difficult still, *faith* is sometimes like an arduous climb where we slow to a crawl and wonder if we can make it to the top. The message of Esther is that God has attached a turbocharger to the engine of our faith that adds tremendous horsepower to our walk with God. With God's turbocharger, we not only can navigate the difficult terrain, we can do so with the speed and energy we need.

The book of Esther superimposes *eight key pathways* over the input-output equation we laid out in "A Different Path" on page 25. These pathways can foster our faith and trust in the Lord. The equation is good. It's like a late model, well-equipped car. It has a great engine and can get us around town. The inputs are the things that allow us to walk with God in such a way that we experience him on a regular basis.

INPUT	OUTPUT
• Study the Bible	• Wisdom/knowledge to live life
• Pray regularly	• Blessings from God
• Fellowship with other believers	• Guidance in your circumstances
• Worship publicly and privately	• Feelings of God's presence
• Serve with your gifts/passions	• Power from the Holy Spirit
• Be generous with your resources	• Motivation to persevere
• Love all people	• Personal character growth

To navigate difficult terrain, however, we need the additional horsepower that comes from ruggedly trusting in God's providence, practicing humility, doing right in the right way, making godly decisions in the storm, creating God room in our plans, living a life of faithfulness to God, tempering our use of power, and celebrating when God moves in unmistakable ways. Superimposed on the input-output equation, it looks like this:

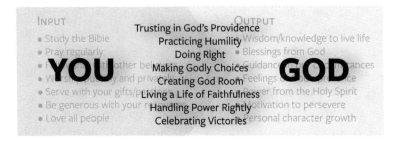

The point is that the things we learn and apply from Esther *don't take the place of our equation, they supplement it.* They add what's needed for us to navigate times of divine distance. They get us to the top of the hill where we can see beautiful vistas of God's presence once again. They worked for Esther, and they can work for us too.

As I wrap up my weekend messages at church, I often say, "I can't wait to see what God does as we follow him in these ways." This is a good way to wrap up our journey as well. I can't wait to see what God does as we navigate seasons of divine distance using the eight tried-and-true ways we have learned in this book. They are a narrow path that leads to life.

REFLECT AND APPLY

Introduction

1. Have you ever experienced the pain of being physically distant from someone important to you? How would you describe that time? What were some of the thoughts and feelings you had when that happened?

2. Have you ever felt distant from God? What were (or are) the circumstances that caused you to feel that God was far away? What are some of the questions you find yourself asking about God (or even to God) when you don't have a sense of his nearness?

3. How does it make you feel to know that you aren't the only one who sometimes feels far away from God?

4. What will it look like for you to be honest about your experience of divine distance and explore what God has available as you navigate it? What are some outcomes you'd like to see as you engage in this effort?

A Different Path

1. Which aspects of the input-output equation do you tend to rely on to get the most out of your faith in

Jesus: Bible study, prayer, fellowship with other believers, public and private worship, serving, generosity, or loving others? In what ways do these things typically bring substance or meaning to your faith?

2. How can you tell when these ways aren't working? What are indicators to you that God feels distant and that your faith feels more fragile than fulfilling?

3. What do you do when these ways don't work? What are some of the things you have done in the past to address the divine distance you were experiencing? How effective have your efforts been? If your results have been underwhelming, why do you think the efforts were ineffective?

4. When you read that the psalmist, the people of Israel, the apostle Paul, and even Jesus himself experienced times of divine distance, what does that tell you about your own struggles?

5. The book of Esther is described as a story where God is at work behind the scenes. How does it encourage you to consider that even if God feels distant, you can have assurance that he's at work in your life, even if it's behind the scenes?

Way 1: Trusting in God's Providence

1. Think about the people in your day-to-day life. What are some of the things that you see them putting their faith in other than God?

2. Who or what is the object of your faith? Have you ever put your faith in something or someone who couldn't

deliver what you expected? What did that look like? What did that do to your faith?

3. How do you experience the truth that faith is a gift of God? In what ways do you treat your faith like it is a gift God has given to you?

4. If Jesus is the object of your faith, what are you trusting in him to do or to be in your life? What do the words *Savior* and *Lord* mean to you? In what ways do these realities serve as a foundation for your faith? What other aspects of your faith depend upon the foundation of Jesus and what he accomplished on the cross?

5. What are the similarities between our culture today and the Persian culture of Esther's time? What are some common popular thoughts or ideas about faith that you hear today that would have been accepted then? Esther's and Mordecai's faith in God's providence was as uncommon then as faith in God's providence is for us today. What does it tell you about God that his ability to provide what is needed in your life doesn't depend on his being popular?

6. How have you seen God's provision over the course of your life? How has that provision been independent of anything you have done?

7. What does it mean to you that "faith is its own experience"? How have you seen this reality to be true in your life? How has faith become its own blessing?

8. In what ways have you seen God's providence give you comfort? How has it given you hope? How has God's providence strengthened you? What are some tangible

ways that trusting in God's providence helps you even when you feel like he is far away?

Way 2: Choosing Humility over Pride

1. Think about a time when your pride was threatened. What were the circumstances? How was your pride threatened?

2. Think about a time when you recognized you were dealing with someone who was truly humble. What caused you to notice their humility? How did their humility affect you?

3. What are some of the ways that pride is celebrated in the culture today? What is the common cultural message or sentiment associated with humility? In what ways does the tension between pride and humility in our culture affect you in your work or your relationships?

4. What does it mean to you that God gives grace to the humble? How have you experienced this in your life? In what ways have you seen this reality at work in the lives of others? How do you think humility can address, or even solve, some of the challenges you are facing?

5. Would other people describe you as a puffer fish or as an angelfish? What would they use to make this assessment?

6. How are you vulnerable to the subtle pull toward pride? In which subtle ways do you tend to find yourself behaving pridefully?

7. What would it look like for you to do a daily audit where you invite God to show you any pride that needs correction? What do you risk in doing this audit? What do you stand to gain?

Way 3: Doing Right in the Right Way

1. When has it been a challenge for you to do the right thing? Have you ever made a moral or ethical compromise? What led you to make that choice? What was the result?

2. What has it looked like in your life for you to bravely choose the right thing even when tempted to make a compromise? What was your standard for making that choice?

3. Have you ever faced negative consequences for doing the right thing? What happened? How did that experience affect you?

4. Where do you see situational ethics exercised in culture today? What are some common justifications given for doing the wrong thing? How does that rationale measure up against a moral code that is rooted in what God has revealed about himself in the Bible?

5. What does it say about your faith when you determine to continue to do the right thing even when God feels distant?

6. How do you think persevering in obedience through spiritually dry seasons can help you feel more of the presence of God?

Way 4: Making Good Decisions in the Storm

1. Have you ever faced your own triple threat, where you were confronted by a tough decision, you wanted to make it in line with God's will, but you weren't at a good place spiritually to discern his will? Describe your triple threat: What was the decision that you had to make? What options were available to you? What caused you to feel that it was difficult to discern God's will at that time? What else complicated the situation for you? Are you facing a triple threat right now?

2. The critical choice facing Esther demonstrates that self-denial and other-centeredness are key to making a tough call. Who are the others who are most at risk or who will benefit most by a tough call that you are facing (or expect to face)? What will it cost you in terms of self-denial to make the tough choice?

3. How do you see self-denial and other-centeredness align with the activity of God throughout history?

4. What are some ways you have happily denied yourself so that others could benefit? What are the variables that cause self-denial to be more difficult?

5. How do you think that providence, humility, doing the right thing, and making good decisions are all related? Can each exist without the others? What happens when one is missing? How do you think these factors—on their own and together—affect your sense of God's nearness or distance?

Way 5: Creating God Room in Your Life

1. What things in your life feel like a well-oiled machine but are really the result of a lot of behind-the-scenes efforts? What would happen if the things being done behind the scenes stopped or changed dramatically?

2. *God room* is creating space in your life for God to do the things that only he can. Have you ever experienced God at work behind the scenes in your life? If so, what happened? At what point did you realize that God had been at work?

3. What is fundamentally necessary for God room? What does making room for God in your circumstances reveal about your sense of God's nature and providence?

4. What are some of the biggest challenges you face in your efforts to create God room? How did Esther address those challenges? What can you do to accomplish similar results?

5. What are some of the challenges you face in your circumstances that are so big that only God can handle them? What are some things you think God might do with the time you intentionally entrust to him? How will your perspective shift if you focus more on God (his attributes, your relationship with him, and his control over your circumstances) than you do on the circumstances themselves?

6. What might it look like for you to wait on God expectantly? What does it look like to actively wait on him from day to day? How would you describe waiting on him joyfully to someone who is unfamiliar with the

effort? What choices do you have to make to wait on God in these three ways?

Way 6: Faithfulness That Delivers

1. Think of someone you'd describe as faithful. What details of their life are present that bring this description to mind? In what ways are they faithful? What have they overcome or avoided to maintain their faithfulness?

2. When in your life have you been tempted to go back on your word, to abandon your beliefs, or to break a promise? If you gave in to that temptation, what compelled you to do so? What do you regret about that choice? If you resisted that temptation, what caused you to remain steadfast? What did your loyalty and faithfulness accomplish? What do you appreciate about the choice you made?

3. Why do you think God values faithfulness? How does faithfulness reflect God's character?

4. Which of the benefits of faithfulness resound most profoundly with you (justice, protection, joy and gladness, evangelism)? How do you think these benefits express God's faithfulness to those affected by them?

5. How do you think persevering in faithfulness even in challenging times or adverse circumstances can help you sense the presence of God? How is faithfulness different from just doubling down in spiritual exercises or disciplines?

6. How have you experienced faithfulness's ability to plow through the roadblocks that this fallen world has put

in your way? What does the experience of overcoming roadblocks tell you about God? What does it tell you about your identity as a child of God?

Way 7: Handling Power

1. What are some of the more obvious ways you have power in your life? In your work? In your home? In your church? In your other relationships? How would others describe your use of power in these contexts?

2. Where in your life do you feel either powerless or greatly disadvantaged with a lack of power? What has happened that has brought this imbalance to your attention? What do you think could be different if you had more power?

3. Evaluate the circumstances where you feel powerless or underpowered. Where do you think you have unrecognized or untapped power available to you through God? Why do you think you have overlooked this power? Might a changed perspective about the power available to you affect whether or not you see yourself as a victim?

4. Do you rightly handle the power you have? How can you handle power better, or more appropriately? What do you think could change? What do you think could change even if your circumstances don't change?

5. What are some of the resources you have available to you to help you control your circumstances, or your actions within your circumstances? Which resources do you tend to rely upon most consistently? Which ones do you tend to overlook or ignore? Why?

6. What will it look like in your relationship dynamics if you temper the power available to you with discipline to use it only defensively, purposefully, and selflessly?

7. What is the risk of power shown without grace? Without truth? Without love? What are some practical ways you can temper your power with grace and truth expressed through love?

8. How will other people in your life flourish with your determination to use power wisely, honorably, and protectively?

Way 8: Celebrating the Victories

1. What are some important events or milestones that are important for you to remember and celebrate? Why? Why do you think it matters for groups of people (spiritual, cultural, ethnic, national) to commemorate and celebrate? What do these celebrations accomplish?

2. What's at risk if these remembrances are abandoned? What happens if people forget what occurred, why it happened, or how it happened?

3. Which aspect of the Jewish celebration of Purim stands out to you as most important: fasting, remembering and reliving our story, feasting, gift exchange, or charitable giving? Why?

4. Why do you think Christians don't celebrate more often?

5. Do you have any Ebenezers or commemorative markers that you use to remember the faithful activity of God in your life? If so, what are they and what do they recall?

If you don't, what could you choose as an Ebenezer? What would it commemorate? Why is it important for you to remember this particular event?

6. How does celebrating to remember and honor help you sense God's nearness? What is accomplished by celebrating spiritually and relationally?

7. What do you like most about celebrating God and his activity in your life? How does intentionally celebrating affect or influence the other times in your life?

Afterword: The Ways Surpass the Formula

1. What do you think it could look like if you apply these eight ways of navigating divine distance to the input-output equation of your spiritual life? How could the activities of your faith life begin to look different? In what ways can you anticipate that they might feel different?

2. How do the eight ways supplement or supercharge your spiritual habits and practices? In what ways do they bring added power for your life's tough conditions? Where do you see God in these ways? How is your sense of God's nearness affected by intentionally walking along these ways as you live out your faith day to day?

3. What are three key takeaways that you've gathered from this book? Why did these stand out to you? What is a concrete way you can apply each of these to your life and circumstances? I encourage you to commit these three intents to God in prayer, thanking him for his

nearness that makes it possible to hear from him even when he feels distant. Thank him that through the power of his Holy Spirit it is possible to persevere in your heartfelt efforts to live by faith in the reality of his providence.

NOTES

Introduction

1. Lisa Firestone, "The Role of Anger in Depression," *Psychology Today*, October 9, 2017, www.psychologytoday.com/us/blog/compassion-matters /201710/the-role-anger-in-depression.

2. Henry David Thoreau, *Walden* (London: Thomas Y. Crowell, 1910), 33.

A Different Path

1. See Pss. 10:1; 13:1; 27:9; 30:7; 44:24; 88:14; 89:46; 102:2; 104:29; and 143:7.

2. C. S. Lewis, *The Joyful Christian* (London: Scribner, 1996), 79.

3. St. John of the Cross, *Dark Night of the Soul* (Mineola, NY: Dover, 2012).

4. D. Martyn Lloyd-Jones, *Spiritual Depression: Its Causes and Cures* (Grand Rapids: Zondervan, 2016).

5. Larry Crabb, *Inside Out* (Colorado Springs: NavPress, 2014).

6. Larry Crabb, *The Pressure's Off: There's a New Way to Live* (Colorado Springs: Waterbrook, 2012), 22.

7. See Gal. 6:9.

8. Exod. 27:21; 28:43; 29:4, 10, 11, 30.

9. Quoted in David M. Howard Jr., *An Introduction to the Old Testament Historical Books* (Chicago: Moody, 2007), 362.

10. Robert Henry Charles, ed., *The Apocrypha and Pseudepigrapha of the Old Testament in English: With Introductions and Critical and Explanatory Notes to the Several Books* (London: Clarendon Press, 1913), 665.

Way 1: Trusting in God's Providence

1. See Rom. 12:3.

2. Mervin Breneman, *Ezra, Nehemiah, Esther: An Exegetical and Theological Exposition of Holy Scripture* (Nashville: Broadman & Holman, 1993), 278, 294.

3. *Holman Bible Dictionary*, s.v. "Providence," by Timothy George, accessed March 1, 2021, https://www.studylight.org/dictionaries/eng/hbd/p/providence.html.
4. Heidelberg Catechism, Lord's Day 1, Q&A 1, WTS Resources, www.students.wts.edu/resources/creeds/heidelberg.html.
5. "Oldest Person to Give Birth," Guinness World Records, 2017, www.guinnessworldrecords.com/world-records/oldest-person-to-give-birth?.
6. Frank Darabont, *The Shawshank Redemption* (screenplay), scene 292, The Daily Script, http://www.dailyscript.com/scripts/shawshank.html.

Way 2 Choosing Humility over Pride

1. Charles Haddon Spurgeon, *Spurgeon's Sermons*, vol. 2 (1856; repr., Ingersoll, Ontario: Devoted Publishing, 2017), 283.

Way 3 Doing Right in the Right Way

1. Randy Alcorn, *The Law of Rewards: Giving What You Can't Keep to Gain What You Can't Lose* (Carol Stream, IL: Tyndale, 2013), ebook, 19.
2. Alcorn, *Law of Rewards*, 20.
3. Randy Alcorn, "An $8.2 Million Judgment and $8.2 Million in Royalties Given Away," Eternal Perspective Ministries (blog), July 1, 2019, www.epm.org/blog/2019/Jul/1/8-million-judgment-royalties.
4. Alcorn, "$8.2 Million Judgment."

Way 4 Making Good Decisions in the Storm

1. See Matt. 16:25.

Way 5 Creating God Room in Your Life

1. Franklin Graham, *Rebel with a Cause: Finally Comfortable Being Graham* (Nashville: Thomas Nelson, 1997), 134–35.
2. Graham, *Rebel with a Cause*, 140.
3. Neil Breneman, *Ezra, Nehemiah, Esther: An Exegetical and Theological Exposition of Holy Scripture*, New American Commentary (Nashville: Holman Reference, 1993), 340.

Way 6 Faithfulness That Delivers

1. Jamie Rasmussen, "The Blessings of Faithfulness," *Nelson's Annual Preacher's Sourcebook*, vol. 4, ed. O. S. Hawkins (Nashville: Thomas Nelson, 2014), 209.
2. M. Alex Johnson, "When You Care Enough to Risk Everything . . . ," NBCNews.com, August 17, 2005, http://www.nbcnews.com/id/8973962/ns/us_news-life/t/when-you-care-enough-risk-everything/#.XuFfNC85RBx.

3. Kim Zetter, "Hackers Finally Post Stolen Ashley Madison Data," *Wired*, June 29, 2017, https://www.wired.com/2015/08/happened-hackers-posted -stolen-ashley-madison-data/.

4. Richard Morgan, "Ashley Madison Is Back—and Claims Surprising User Numbers," *New York Post*, May 21, 2017, https://nypost.com/2017/05 /21/ashley-madison-is-back-and-claims-surprising-user-numbers/.

Way 7 Handling Power

1. Gen. 18:14; 2 Sam. 22:33; 2 Chron. 14:11; Pss. 62:11; 66:7; 68:35; 147:4–5; Isa. 40:29, 31; Jer. 10:12; 32:17; Zeph. 3:17.

2. Matt. 28:18–20; Acts 1:8.

3. John 15:5; Gal. 6:5.

4. 2 Cor. 12:9–10; Eph. 6:10; Phil. 4:13; Col. 1:11; Heb. 11:34.

5. Rom. 15:13; 2 Cor. 13:11; 2 Tim. 1:7; 2 Pet. 1:3.

6. "H7980—Shalat—Strong's Hebrew Lexicon (KJV)," Blue Letter Bible, accessed July 22, 2020, https://www.blueletterbible.org/lang/lexicon/lexicon .cfm?Strongs=H7980.

7. F. Engel De Janösi, "The Correspondence between Lord Acton and Bishop Creighton," *Cambridge Historical Journal* 6, no. 3 (1940): 307–21.

8. "Thomas Jefferson to Thomas Leiper, 12 June 1815," *Founders Online* (collection), National Archives, accessed June 18, 2020, https://founders .archives.gov/documents/Jefferson/03-08-02-0431.

Jamie Rasmussen (MDiv, Trinity Evangelical Divinity School) is the senior pastor of Scottsdale Bible Church, which over the course of his leadership since 2007 has been regularly included in *Outreach Magazine*'s annual list of the top 100 largest and fastest growing churches. Having served as an ordained pastor for more than thirty years, Jamie has pastored churches in Detroit, Michigan; London, Ontario; Chagrin Falls, Ohio; and Scottsdale, Arizona. He is the author of *How Joyful People Think* (Baker Books, 2018).

The secret to getting the most out of life is within your reach.

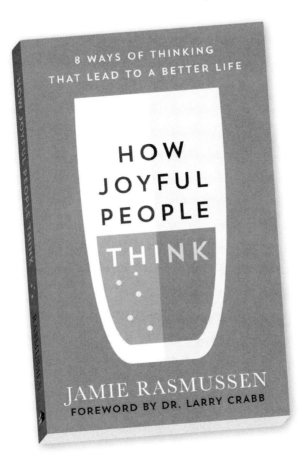

In this insightful unpacking of Philippians 4:8, pastor Jamie Rasmussen shows readers how to focus their thoughts and attention on the things in life that God has declared will make a meaningful impact on both a person's outlook and experience. It's the kind of thinking that has the power to change us, pointing us away from self-pity, anger, and resentment and toward contentment and personal peace, which helps us get the most out of life.